Cumbrian Communities and their Railways No 5

Millom

A Cumberland Iron Town and its Railways

Alan Atkinson

CUMBRIAN RAILWAYS ASSOCIATION

Other publications by the Cumbrian Railways Association

'Cumbrian Communities' Series:
- No 1   Grange-over-Sands *(Leslie R Gilpin)* - Out of print
- No 2   Ravenglass *(Peter van Zeller)* - Out of print
- No 3   Dalton-in-Furness *(Rock Battye)*
- No 4   Whitehaven *(Howard Quayle)*

'Railway Histories' Series:
- The Kendal & Windermere Railway *(Dick Smith)* - Out of print
- The Furness Railway in and around Barrow *(Dr Michael Andrews)* - Out of print
- The Coniston Railway *(Dr Michael Andrews & Geoff Holme)*
- The Track of the Ironmasters *(W McGowan Gradon - edited by Peter Robinson)*
- The Ulverstone & Lancaster Railway *(Leslie R Gilpin)*

Photographic Albums:
- A Cumbrian Railway Album *(Leslie R Gilpin)*

Locomotive Histories:
- The Great Survivor *(Tim Owen)*

Other Titles:
- Railwaymen of Cumbria Remembered - A Roll of Honour

Text © 2012 Alan Atkinson and the Cumbrian Railways Association

Maps © Alan Johnstone and the Cumbrian Railways Association

Photographs © from Cumbrian Railways Association Photo Library and as credited

**Published by the Cumbrian Railways Association,
104 Durley Avenue, Pinner, Middlesex HA5 1JH**

**The Association is Registered Charity No 1025436
www.cumbrianrailways.org.uk**

Membership Secretary, Cumbrian Railways Association, Alan Crawford,
95 Harrington Road, Workington, Cumbria CA14 2UE

Design and layout by Michael Peascod

Printed by The Amadeus Press Ltd, Cleckheaton

ISBN 978-0-9570387-1-4

All rights reserved. No part of this publication may be reproduced, stored in a retrieval system or transmitted in any form or by any means, electronic, mechanical, photocopying, recording or otherwise without prior permission in writing from the publisher.

The Cumbrian Railways Association is the local railway history group for Cumbria and North Lancashire. With a membership of over 420 it is a registered charity with the aim of promoting interest in and knowledge of the railways of this area, and the part they have played in its development over the last 150 years. For more information about the Association, its activities and services, please visit our website at www.cumbrianrailways.org.uk or write to the Membership Secretary at the above address.

Contents

	Introduction	5
1	Pre-Industrial Millom (1086 - 1860)	7
2	The Arrival of the Railway (1835 - 1866)	11
3	Hodbarrow - a Great Mine (1855 - 1968)	27
4	Millom Ironworks (1867 - 1968)	41
5	The New Town (1866 onwards)	59
6	The Furness Railway takes over (1866 - 1923)	69
7	The Railway after 1923	93
	Appendix 1 - LMS Strip Map	105
	Appendix 2 - The Rescue of Millom Ironworks No 1	106
	Bibliography	109
	Index	111

St George's church is prominent on the skyline as FR 0-6-0 52494 takes empty ore wagons back to West Cumberland on Moor Row trip 99. This 4th September 1953 view is taken from Church Walk which connects Moor Road bridge with St George's Road bridge.
Photo: VR Webster/Kidderminster Railway Museum

Front Cover and Frontispiece
In the 1960s the Hodbarrow Mining Company's 1890-built Neilson crane tank 'Snipey' is busy loading pit props against a background of Millom Ironworks and Newtown.
From a painting by Alan Gunston

Introduction

IN ATTEMPTING to compile a history of Millom and its railways one must first ask the question, "where is Millom?" The answer is nowhere near as simple as "a small post-industrial town at the mouth of the River Duddon", for it depends on whether one is referring to the Lordship, civil parish, township, Urban District, Rural District or just the current town. For the purposes of this historical narrative Millom will be all of these and more besides: the author hopes that it is clear from the context to which he is referring. This volume covers the railways between the Duddon and the Esk and considers in some detail the industry and commercial development of the principal settlement in the area.

Millom is not a "railway town" in the same sense as Crewe or Swindon but it is undoubtedly true that, without the railway, the new town which appeared during the latter part of the nineteenth century to the south of the Whitehaven & Furness Junction line would never have been built. Millom, or Newtown as it continued to be called by the residents of Holborn Hill well into the twentieth century, is a product of the nineteenth-century iron industry and, without the railway, the mine at Hodbarrow could never have achieved the size it did nor would the ironworks ever have been built where it was. The building of the railway to Hodbarrow necessitated the construction of an embankment on the banks of the Duddon and it was this embankment that enabled the marshy ground to be drained in order to build the town. Both iron companies were to have an unprecedented influence on the social and economic development of this remote area of south Cumberland but it was the railway which reduced the isolation of a part of the county that had not shared in the benefits of earlier road improvements.

Late twentieth-century commentators have not been kind to Millom: Millward and Robinson in The Regions of Britain -The Lake District (1970) described the town as "a starkly simple ore-mining and smelting centre whose cycle of history is already completed"; the Mayor of Copeland infamously called it "a place of despair" and even the town's most famous son, the writer and poet Norman Nicholson, referred to the place as "a decaying Victorian settlement" in Greater Lakeland (1969). Today's visitor could be forgiven for sympathising with these sentiments, but to do so is to misunderstand Millom's significance as the site of the largest haematite deposit in the United Kingdom and the centre of a consistently prosperous and innovative iron manufacturing industry.

I was brought up in Millom and spent much time watching trains around the station and goods yard: my final year of primary education and all secondary years were spent within sight of the railway and only when it was almost too late did I take more than a passing interest in the extensive industrial systems at Hodbarrow and the ironworks. I hope that this book, with its focus on the history and influence of the railways, both main line and industrial, will be a worthy addition to the few publications about the town.

Alan Atkinson
Worcestershire, 2012

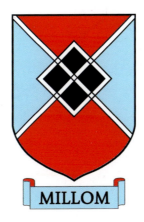

Map drawn by Alan Johnstone.

Pre-Industrial Millom (1086-1860)

The Lords of Millom; an agricultural economy; early haematite mining; the Duddon Furnace; mining at The Hill; communications before the railway.

"A marshy, muddy, sand-and-shingle peninsula, moored like a raft between the mouth of the River Duddon and the Irish Sea."
　　　　　　　　Norman Nicholson, 'Wednesday Early Closing'

AT THE TIME of the Norman Conquest much of Cumberland had been overrun by the Scots and only the south-western tip of the county around Millom appears in the Domesday Survey of 1086. The survey shows that the country on either side of the Duddon estuary belonged to the huge manor of Hougon, containing most of Low Furness as well as estates at Bootle, Whicham and Kirksanton. Between 1096 and 1100 the first Lord of Millom, Godard de Boyvill, was invested by Ranulf le Meschin who owned the greater part of Cumberland and much of Westmorland. In 1120 Henry I granted the Barony of Egremont, or Copeland, to William le Meschin, Ranulf's brother, and the Millom seignory was the most extensive lordship within the barony including, as it did, the parishes of Millom, Bootle, Corney, Waberthwaite, Whicham and Whitbeck. This seignory, which was to all intents and purposes a separate unit from the Egremont Lordship, possessed great privileges: its lords enjoyed *jura regalia*, the power to execute without trial, in the six parishes and it was a special jurisdiction into which the Sheriff of the County could not enter. The last occasion on which this power of life or death was exercised in Millom was in the early seventeenth century and in Victorian times a stone was erected to mark the spot where executions took place: the Gallows Stone is close to the railway about ½ mile north east of the station.

As was customary during medieval times, the de Boyvills later took the name de Millom (alternative spellings were Milham, Millome, Mullum, Millam, Mylum or Millum). By 1125 the de Boyvills had started to build Millom Castle together with the adjacent church and, during the following hundred years, four generations of the family enjoyed the privileges and responsibilities of the Lordship of Millom. The early development of the parish was closely connected with Furness Abbey, which was founded in 1127, and the monks established salt works on the Cumberland bank of the Duddon, still remembered in Salthouse Road and Salthouse Farm. The last de Boyvill at Millom was Joan, the daughter of Adam, and she brought the Lordship to John Huddleston when she married him around 1240. For the next five hundred years the Huddlestons were to literally hold the power of life or death over the inhabitants of the district.

In 1251 Henry III gave Sir John Huddleston a charter for a market every Wednesday and for a three-day fair every year at Trinitytide. A fair was the most important franchise that could be annexed to a manor: here tenants could sell their goods and purchase wares which they could not produce themselves but, unfortunately, the Lord of Millom died before paying for his privilege and his successor was sued for the money. Both market and fair were eventually to lapse: Nicholson & Burn, writing in 1777, said the market "hath been long discontinued" but it was later revived during the rapid growth of the new town in the latter half of the nineteenth century. The fair was not revived.

The Huddlestons were to steer the Manor of Millom through some very difficult times, starting with raids by the Scots during most of the fourteenth century, following the defeat of the English at Bannockburn in 1314. Two years later the Manor at Kirksanton (the Lords of Kirksanton were a branch of the de Boyvill family) was burned during one such raid when, according to the *Larnercost Chronicles*, the Scots "laid waste to everything as far as Furness . . . taking away men and women as prisoners". In 1322 Robert the Bruce headed another savage raid and this led to a spate of castle building and rebuilding which included Muncaster, Irton, Millom, Piel and Gleaston. Millom Castle was built in a strategic position on a small hillock adjacent to the road which led from the principal Duddon ford to The Street, the ancient road which ran under Black Combe past Whicham (Whittyham or Whittecham in the 17th century), Whitbeck (Whidbeck) and Bootle (Bowtell) churches to the ford across the Esk by Waberthwaite. The land surrounding the castle was described as "a peaty morass . . . crossed by stepping stones" and the high spring tides would have lapped round the hillock prior to the nineteenth century reclamation of the Duddon flats. John Huddleston was granted the King's licence to enclose the castle with a moat and to crenellate (fortify) it in 1335, but it was not until a little over a hundred years later that the defences were put to the test when the castle was partly destroyed, not by Scots but by Lancastrians, during the Wars of the Roses.

Some two hundred years later the Huddlestons were on the wrong side in another conflict which resulted in their castle being destroyed. The Civil War of 1642 found the gentry of the district divided with the bulk of the people for Parliament. Colonel Sir William Huddleston raised a regiment for the King but in 1643 was beaten by an inferior force of Parliamentarians at Lindal Close (the ridge overlooking Lindal Cote) within 15 minutes of

Old Church and Castle, Millom.

Millom Castle appears as an almost ghostly presence behind the east end of Holy Trinity church in this postcard sent in 1903. The proximity of the two buildings is apparent and, whilst the castle is little more than a ruin converted into a farm, the church still serves its original function, albeit having being rebuilt on numerous occasions and now joined with St George's church in the unified Parish of Millom.

Photo: Author's Collection

Chapter One

This 1912 view of Borwick Rails harbour looking north shows the tidal area between and behind the two iron companies' piers. The vessel in the centre is moored at the ironworks pier and the Hodbarrow tug, Duddon, *is at the end of the mining company's pier. The tug's funnel may be seen to the left of the large shed. The coming of the railway in 1850 virtually put this natural harbour out of business until the first cargo from Hodbarrow was shipped from here in 1859. Photo: Bill Myers Collection*

the battle beginning. Many were drowned attempting to retreat across the Duddon sands, while Colonel Huddleston and 400 of his men were captured and taken prisoner. In the following year the castle was besieged by the Parliamentary army and, despite obstinate resistance, was captured and slighted. Sir William died in a debtor's prison and from then on each lord was saddled with the debts of his predecessor. As had happened with the de Boyvills before them, the Huddleston era ended with a daughter as heir. Elizabeth Huddleston married Sir Hedworth Williamson, who in 1774 sold the Millom estate to Sir James Lowther, afterwards Earl of Lonsdale, for £20,000 (over £2,000,000 at today's prices), the proceeds being used to pay the debts of the last two lords. The advertisement for the sale in the *St James Chronicle* described the "well stocked deer park, . . . about 1,500 acres of demesne lands, . . . together with free chase and free warren over a very considerable tract of country between the rivers Duddon and Esk . . . ".

Sir James did not acquire a great bargain, for, as long ago as 1688, Thomas Denton wrote that "the castle was much out of repair". A view of the castle published in 1739 represents the building in much the same ruinous state as it presents today. Since the fourteenth century deer had been kept in fenced parks but Millom's new owner, concerned over rising costs, finally disparked the estate around 1802 when some 207 deer were killed and the venison sold in Ulverston market. The park was apportioned to various farms but the name *Millom Park* remains, albeit referring to a much smaller area than the pre-nineteenth-century enclosure.

At the beginning of the nineteenth century the area close to the mouth of the Duddon was described as low-lying and ill-drained with the only habitation being in isolated farms, such as Bracken Hill (on the site of the later schools in Lapstone Road), Old Rottington House (opposite the later Peel Hotel), New Rottington House (on what was later Lonsdale Road), Lapstone Lodge (near the junction of the later Lancashire Road and Lapstone Road) and Borwick Rails. There were numerous farms, many of which still stand, dotted about the higher ground inland from the sea and throughout the huge parish of Millom, which extended some 18 miles from the Duddon in the south to the Esk in the north. In 1688 this far-flung parish contained merely 900 persons and this had risen to only 1,502 by 1801, with 589 souls living in the township of Millom, comprising Lower Millom and Upper Millom. Given the proximity of the sea, it is not surprising that fishing was noted in the area as early as 1338 and the estuary was renowned for its mussels, cockles, salmon and sand eels. Sandford, writing in 1675, speaks of the Duddon as "a brave river, where the famous cockles of all England is gathered in the sands, scraped out with hooks like sickles, and brave salmons and flookes, the bravest in England, hung up and dried like bacon". As late as 1877 the Furness Railway forwarded 343 tons of cockles from Millom over the year. Fishing was recorded at Borwick Rails (Barret Ralys, Burick Rails, Burwick-Rails, Burrow Crails or Barwick Rails) in the fourteenth century but by the early nineteenth century this natural harbour at the mouth of the three small creeks (Salt Home Pool, Rottington Pool and Crook Pool) was being used to export slate (its main traffic), corn, wood for basket making, etc. and for importing coal. The curiously-named Borwick Rails has nothing to do with railways: Frank Warriner, in *Millom People and Places,* claims that it is derived from the Old English *berewick*, meaning demesne farm. In the early nineteenth century the majority of people were employed on the land or in associated jobs such as blacksmiths, wheelwrights or in the sickle factory at White Hall in Whicham Valley. Wheat, barley, oats and turnips were grown and, prior to 1800, villagers at Kirksanton grew hemp for the rope walk there: slate pencils were made at Arnaby, while at Thwaites there were woollen mills dating back to the sixteenth century and which were still working in the early part of the twentieth century. *Lewis's Topographical Dictionary of England* observed in 1831 that "mineral productions are limestone, slate and iron and copper ore; the limestone alone is found in sufficient quantities to be worked to advantage".

Iron, as will be seen in later chapters, runs like a thread though Millom's history. The earliest remains of the iron industry between the Esk and the Duddon are those of bloomeries (primitive furnaces in which burning charcoal reduced iron ore to a bloom of iron) dating from Romano-British and early mediaeval times which were discovered to the west of Eskmeals (Old Norse, meaning sand dunes at the mouth of the Esk) station. It is thought that ore was shipped in by sea from Egremont or Furness and that there may have been large amounts of timber available thereabouts. The process, which changed little for over a thousand years, involved bringing small charges of ore by packhorse and heating it with charcoal for several hours, more or less reducing it so that it could be forged into bars of iron. The demand for timber was prodigious and, by the middle of the sixteenth century, most of the large timber in the area had been felled in order to produce charcoal for this process. William Huddleston (died 1628) mentions his

Pre-Industrial Millom (1086-1860)

furnace at Ulpha and Ferdinand Huddleston, writing in 1688, refers to men working in the mines (which turned out to be unsuccessful). Thomas Denton, also writing in 1688, records that £4,000 worth of oak had been cut down to supply forges in Millom parish within the previous 30 years. Some of the iron ore deposits came to the surface, but as early as 1718 it is recorded that several hundred tons of ore had been taken from the pits at Millom and in 1731 William Huddleston was advertising leases on lead, iron, coal and copper in the Lordship of Millom. Leases were again advertised in 1770 but without the coal option and, perhaps signifying a lack of interest, "great encouragement will be given to work the same". Furnace Beck, which runs through Ghyll Scaur (to the north-east of Millom, near The Hill), has slag heap remains alongside it, indicating small scale iron manufacture in the area.

The largest remains of the pre-nineteenth century iron industry in the old Millom parish are at the Duddon Furnace which was established close to Duddon Bridge in 1737 by the Cunsey and Backbarrow Companies. The site was well chosen as there were extensive coppice woods surrounding it and power was derived from the fast-flowing Duddon. The Backbarrow Company sold its shares to its erstwhile partner in 1741; from 1763 William Latham, the former manager, owned the ironworks and the business was acquired by Harrison, Ainslie & Company in 1829. Regular shipments of iron ore from the Furness mines were shipped in shallow-draughted sloops from Ireleth Marsh to the wharf on Lady Hall Marsh, just below Duddon Bridge and about a mile from the furnace. Similarly, the finished product was shipped out via the same route, although in later years pig iron was shipped from the harbour at Borwick Rails. As already noted, one of the major problems with early iron production was the copious quantity of wood required to produce charcoal for the reduction of the haematite; the Duddon Furnace needed charcoal from ten acres of coppice every week and so was not always in blast if fuel stocks were low. As early as 1775 the Cunsey Company built a furnace on the shores of Loch Fyne in Scotland because of the shortage of charcoal in Cumberland. In 1783 Henry Cort invented the puddling furnace and thereafter cheap iron from this source ousted bar iron. The Industrial Revolution, however, increased the demand for iron and, despite Abraham Darby's success at producing iron from coke in Coalbrookdale in 1709, the technically obsolete charcoal-fired furnace survived to meet this demand. In any case there were no coal reserves in Furness and the West Cumberland coal was remote and considered unsuited to making coke at that time – a problem that was to become even more significant in later years. The Duddon Furnace struggled on until it finally closed down sometime between 1867 and 1871, just as the modern ironworks with its coke-fired blast furnaces further down the Duddon at Borwick Rails was starting production. The site has been a Scheduled Ancient Monument since 1963 and contains possibly the most complete surviving charcoal-fired blast furnace in England.

There was a revival of mining activity in Millom Above township following the discovery of iron ore on the High Brow estate of John Shepherd at The Hill in 1848, and throughout the 1850s prospectors searched for other ore bodies in the Coniston Limestone rocks below Millom Park. From 1851 small scale mining of pyrite (iron sulphide), from which sulphur could be extracted and sulphuric acid produced, also went on at High Brow; around 30 men are known to have been employed at the works in 1858. A wharf was opened at Underhill alongside the Whitehaven & Furness Junction Railway in 1854. In November 1856 a new company commenced operations near the castle by reopening an existing pit to exploit a bed of ore some 30ft thick and in 1857 the Millom Mining Company was incorporated, using London finance, to purchase the existing grants at Waterblean, near The Hill. This venture was led by James Davis (1808-1895), a former partner of Henry Schneider (1817-1887) in the Park mine on the opposite side of the estuary and who had also tried his luck at Hodbarrow. Schneider had arrived in Barrow in 1839, had discovered the fabulously rich Park deposit in 1851 and in 1859 opened the first blast furnaces at Hindpool. While Schneider went on to be a founding partner with James Ramsden in the Furness Railway and the Barrow Haematite Iron and Steel Company, Davis seems to have been consistently in the right place at the wrong time. He pulled out of the Park venture just as it was becoming successful (it was the greatest haematite deposit in British history until the discovery of the Hodbarrow ore body) and abandoned his search at Hodbarrow, thereby allowing Nathaniel Caine and John Barratt to eventually discover and work the extensive deposits there, as described in Chapter 3. The *Ulverston Advertiser* reported on 7th September 1854 that about 30 workmen and others in the employ of Davis at the mines at Underhill sat down to a supper at the White Horse Inn, at which event Davis optimistically announced that "in the course of time he hoped to have a much larger number of men employed; in fact the district showed every symptom of rich mineral deposit, and he would leave nothing undone to discover the real mineral wealth of the district". Davis was so nearly right but he would not be employing the men as he was prospecting about three miles too far north. Davis was reported as having installed the first engine working underground in the area in 1858 some 180ft below the surface but, sadly, the optimism was unfounded and the "valuable and extensive mineral grant of haematite iron ore royalty . . . in the neighbourhood of the great

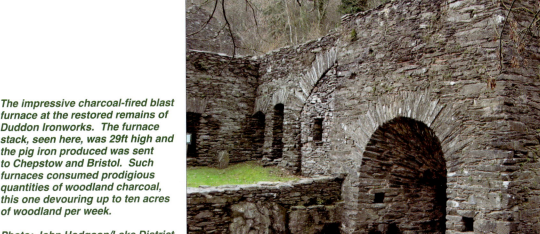

The impressive charcoal-fired blast furnace at the restored remains of Duddon Ironworks. The furnace stack, seen here, was 29ft high and the pig iron produced was sent to Chepstow and Bristol. Such furnaces consumed prodigious quantities of woodland charcoal, this one devouring up to ten acres of woodland per week.

Photo: John Hodgson/Lake District National Park Authority

Chapter One

This early twentieth century view looking east from the top of Main Street, Holborn Hill, shows something of the character of the pre-Newtown era. Today it would not be sensible to stand in the same place to take a photograph: despite through traffic being diverted away from Holborn Hill, there would be more than a lone cyclist with which to contend.

Photo: Author's Collection

producing mines of Hodbarrow" was advertised for sale in the *Liverpool Mercury* of 17th February 1869. The Millom Mining Company, whose directors included Caine and James Barratt, was dissolved on 16th April 1870.

A pit had been sunk at Waterblean around 1864 by James Barratt, Nathaniel Caine and John Tyson, the latter being listed as the proprietor and Barratt as manager. Haematite was discovered but the ruddle (red ocherous ore) thereabouts was of little value except for smit (smit marks were used to distinguish the farm and owner of sheep) and the production of paint, although three shafts were sunk and a reasonable barytes (barium sulphate) deposit was also worked. The tonnage raised was never great, the ore had to be carted a considerable distance and, as Hodbarrow developed, the mine was abandoned in 1881, by which date the owner was George Eveson and the agent Ezekiel Dawson. The Waterblean Colour & Mining Company, in which the Cumberland Iron Mining & Smelting Company (see Chapter 5) had shares, took over the works around 1890; extensive surface modifications were made and an expensive plant for the manufacture of paint was constructed. The same problems of inaccessibility hampered the new enterprise; the company was wound up in 1899 and the machinery sold off on 27th July that year. It is possible that some small scale production of paint went on until the 1920s.

Located between the high ground of Cumbria and the sea, the parish of Millom was isolated from much of the rest of the country, and communications were poor before the arrival of the Whitehaven & Furness Junction Railway in 1850. Alone among the towns of Cumberland, Millom experienced its most rapid population growth after the arrival of the railway and, as late as 1870, the recently-appointed County Road Surveyor considered the Millom and Bootle roads to be the worst kept and least important of any he had examined. The Egremont to Salthouse Turnpike Trust received its Act of Parliament in 1750 but the planned route south to the Cumberland bank of the Duddon was never constructed, although the Kirkby Kendal to Kirkby Ireleth Trust was established in 1763 and the turnpike built, leading to the crossing of the Duddon sands known as the Low Ford. The road formerly known as Main Street (now Holborn Hill) follows the course of the eighteenth-century west coast route and still contains the few inns and cottages remaining which predate mid-Victorian Millom. A plaque on a house in Holborn Hill marks the location of the Pilot Inn, where a stone above the door reads

William and Ann Farren live heare. Who mostly keep good ale and beer 1745. You that intend to cross Ye Sand call here a Gide att your command.

Guides to cross the sands could be hired but, by the time that the railway arrived, they were no longer available and deaths by drowning were averaging about one a year. The regular carriers and carters marked the road across the sands with branches of broom, which they altered as the sands shifted. There were other fords that could be traversed at low tide, one of which, the Middle Ford, joined Sandside, near Kirkby, to the Cumberland shore close to the site of the later Underhill Station and another, the High Ford, linked Sandside with the road to The Green, crossing the later railway at Green Road station. Whilst the early newspapers carried many accounts of people crossing the sands and being caught by the incoming tide, this route remained in common use until well after the railway had arrived. In his diary for 12th May 1759 John Wesley wrote "we came to Bottle (Bootle) . . . soon after eight, having crossed the Millam Sand, without either guide or difficulty" and many of those flocking to seek their fortunes at the new mines or at the ironworks would have travelled this way, rather than by the long road through Broughton and over Duddon Bridge. By 1810 the road from Salthouse to the castle had been built and, following the 1820 Millom Enclosure Act, the Earl of Lonsdale had, by 1830, reclaimed 250 acres of Arnaby Moss (otherwise waste land) from the Duddon estuary by the construction of the Millom Embankment at a cost of nearly £3,000. The Act permitted up to 1,000 acres to be enclosed up to mid-stream and, although this latter was never done, the eventual construction of the railway between Millom and Foxfield was made much more straightforward by the building of the embankment.

In 1821 the township of Lower Millom, comprising mainly Holborn Hill and several detached houses, had a population of only 320. Upper Millom, comprising The Hill and The Green, exceeded this at 460; Ulpha was recorded at 368 and Chapel Sucken, made up of Haverigg and Kirksanton, contained 251 inhabitants. Out of the 155 households listed in Millom at this time, 109 were involved in agricultural work. Confusingly, in view of subsequent developments in the 1860s, maps published in the eighteenth and early nineteenth centuries refer to a small collection of dwellings between Holborn Hill and the Duddon ford as *Millom New Town*. The novelist Elizabeth Gaskell spent some time in Holborn Hill in 1851 and, singularly unimpressed, wrote "it was built on the side of a hill, of old grey stone houses, with certain appendages in the way of dirty ponds". By then Lower Millom was referred to as *Millom Below* and contained no more than 416 persons, while Upper Millom, by then *Millom Above,* had 564. *The English Cyclopaedia 1854* describes Millom as "a place of no consequence" but unwittingly hints at future prosperity when it adds "there is a small fishery and mines in the neighbourhood". *Kelly's Cumberland Directory* describes the area before 1860 as "smiling under its weight of golden grain or forming luxuriant pastures on which the cattle lazily browsed" and *The Philologist* said of Holborn Hill "there is a good inn and one or two small lodging houses. It is frequented chiefly by the commercial traveller, the sportsman and an occasional antiquarian or geologist". How this bucolic scene was to change over the coming ten years!

The Arrival of the Railway (1835-1866)

London to Scotland via Millom; the Whitehaven & Furness Junction Railway; the Duddon viaduct saga; stormy relationships with the Furness Railway.

"If you do not bring forward this line of railway, and support it with all your might, West Cumberland will forever after remain in the back settlements".

John Urpeth Rastrick, 'Report to the Provisional Committee of the West Cumberland, Furness & Morecambe Bay Railway'

THE FIRST proposals for a railway round the Cumbrian coast came from the notable engineer, linguist and author Hyde Clarke (1815-1895) in 1835. He proposed the Grand Caledonian Junction Railway, which would form a route from Preston, through Lancaster and Dumfries to Glasgow and Edinburgh, crossing Morecambe Bay and the Duddon by embankments. Clarke and Richard Julian were to be the engineers for the scheme. The railway would be virtually level, 39,210 acres would be reclaimed by the ten mile embankment across Morecambe Bay and 4,000 acres would be enclosed by the three mile Duddon embankment, with the capital returned on the reclaimed land being estimated at over £1 million. Since the whole 190 miles were estimated to cost £2,969,065, the significance of the land reclaimed is obvious and this argument would be used again in later schemes that involved crossing both tracts of water. After preliminary surveys at Clarke's expense, a local committee was formed at Whitehaven. The driving force behind the scheme, Sir Humphrey Le Fleming Senhouse (c1778–1841) of Seascale Hall, stated at the time that "if this railroad were fairly in operation West Cumberland would become a great manufacturing mart". Sir Humphrey's grandfather, another Humphrey Senhouse (1705-1770), had founded the town of Maryport, naming it after his wife Mary, and so his grandson may well have had an interest in bringing the railway to the town. Le Fleming Senhouse was a captain in the Royal Navy whose influence on railway politics in West Cumberland was to come to an abrupt end on his death from fever on board HMS *Blenheim* at Hong Kong.

The committee of the proposed Grand Caledonian Junction Railway, supported by the Rt Hon William Lowther the First Earl of Lonsdale (1757-1844), asked George Stephenson (1781-1848) on 1st September 1836 to report on a line to Scotland via the West Cumberland coast but unfortunately he was too busy at the time to undertake this work. On 6th June 1837 the committee of the proposed Whitehaven, Workington & Maryport Railway (part of the Grand Caledonian project) again approached Stephenson with a view to completing a line of railway from London to Glasgow and Edinburgh. He was requested to make an "ocular survey" of a route between Lancaster and Carlisle via Ulverston and Whitehaven and an alternative route via Kirkby Lonsdale and Penrith. Stephenson started his survey on 1st August 1837, when he examined Morecambe Bay and crossed the sands to Ulverston. The following day he examined the Furness peninsula and looked for a possible route north via Coniston or Windermere. He then crossed the Duddon sands and travelled around Black Combe to Ravenglass, from where he followed the coast to Whitehaven and made a foray inland from Egremont to Cockermouth. Arriving at Carlisle, he followed the River Petteril to Penrith, climbed over Shap Fell and reached Lancaster via Kirkby Lonsdale on 10th August. Having covered an enormous tract of the North West in ten days, he produced his report just six days later; one is forced to wonder about the depth of such a brief survey or whether Stephenson was really interested in either scheme.

In his report he proposed to cross Morecambe Bay on a curved embankment from Poulton-le-Sands (later Morecambe) to Humphrey Head, carrying on through Pennington to Kirkby Ireleth via a deep cutting and tunnel. After crossing the Duddon sands from Dunnerholme on a 1¾ mile embankment, the

All the various west coast schemes utilised the easy terrain between the sea and the hills and fells of the western Lake District. On 17th August 1957 Fowler 2P 4-4-0 40654 and Stanier 4MT 2-6-4T 42560 approach Limestone Hall crossing as they head south.
Photo: VR Webster/Kidderminster Railway Museum

Chapter Two

Despite having few gradients, one of the disadvantages of the coastal route was the large number of viaducts required. Two DRS Class 20s and a Class 37 bring a nuclear flask train south from Sellafield over the River Esk on 15th August 2002. The ensemble will shortly pass the site of Eskmeals station.
Photo: Alan Johnstone Ref 3393

proposed route would travel parallel to the shore, but about a mile inland, to Bootle and then directly to Ravenglass, Drigg and St Bees. It would then turn inland to reach Whitehaven, before following the coast to Workington and on to Maryport. There it would join the Maryport & Carlisle Railway, already surveyed in detail by himself and which had gained its Act on 12th July 1837. Stephenson claimed that the route from Lancaster to Maryport was almost dead level and was nowhere more than 40 feet above sea level. He was of the view (which, in the event, turned out to be correct) that the Whitehaven-Duddon portion would be cheaper than most railways to construct and that the cost of the expensive portions over the Duddon estuary and across Morecambe Bay would be more than compensated for by the value of the land reclaimed (although this latter premise was, of course, never tested).

Not surprisingly, given that west coast interests had commissioned him to prepare the report, Stephenson gave little consideration to the alternative route via Penrith, considering that the gradients, tunnelling and expense weighed heavily against it. The coast route, on the other hand, would be easier to work and free from snow, although he did accept that the distance would be greater. "Old George" did not attach any estimates of costs to his report although he suggested that reclaimed land would offset the cost of building the railway. The committee estimated a figure of £341,500 for the 49½ miles from Lancaster to Whitehaven.

Stephenson later claimed that the report had been published to raise money for the work and that the directors had left out his comments that the Morecambe Bay embankment was too big a project for any company without government assistance. Consequent upon this omission, he resigned from the project. In an 1839 report to the Preston & Wyre Railway he suggested that, if the government would not take on the Morecambe Bay project, the Cumberland people should construct a harbour on the Duddon, from which ships could connect to Fleetwood to provide a through route to Scotland. However, by this time events had moved on.

Following the receipt of Stephenson's report the Cumbrians did nothing until, in January 1838, a newly formed committee, representing the proposed West Cumberland, Furness & Morecambe Bay Railway, received an offer from the secretary of the Preston & Wyre Railway to fund the survey of a railway from Maryport to Rampside, there to connect with the Wyre route by steamers across Morecambe Bay. The proviso was that the West Cumberland committee advanced £500 towards the survey. Le Fleming Senhouse was once more in the chair and his committee obviously had grander ideas; they declined the Preston & Wyre's offer and promptly gave instructions to John Hague (c1781-1857) to report on the crossing of Morecambe Bay and the Duddon estuary. Hague, who had been involved in building sea dykes in Holland and drainage schemes in Lincolnshire and Cambridgeshire, was recommended by Senhouse's friend Colonel Moody RE. By November 1838 Hague had completed his report and submitted it to the committee on the 27th of that month. The committee resolved to accept the report although the *Cumberland Pacquet* was of the view that "public feeling was on the decline". In contrast to Stephenson's more modest plans, which he considered impracticable, Hague recommended an embankment straight across Morecambe Bay, some 10 miles 51 chains in length: the Duddon crossing would be 1 mile 65 chains from Roanhead Crag to Hodbarrow Point. The two embankments would carry a double line of railway and the estimated cost of the scheme was £434,131 9s 4d (how the early engineers loved such exact estimates!) which was about the same as the earlier committee had reckoned for the whole line to Maryport after receiving Stephenson's report. Like him, Hague considered that land reclamation would offset capital expenditure and estimated that 46,300 acres would be reclaimed in Morecambe Bay and 5,700 acres in the Duddon estuary, yielding income of £1,196,000 at £23 per acre. Piles 21ft apart would be sunk in four rows across Morecambe Bay and the Duddon and these would be capped with longitudinal and diagonal timbers. Wooden sheeting piles would be driven down to keep the water back, with stones tipped from wagons on the track laid on top of the wooden structure. On the seaward side of the embankments Hague proposed to construct a bank six feet high to protect trains from wind and spray and calculated that it would take only 18 months to complete the Duddon crossing.

The Arrival of the Railway (1835 - 1866)

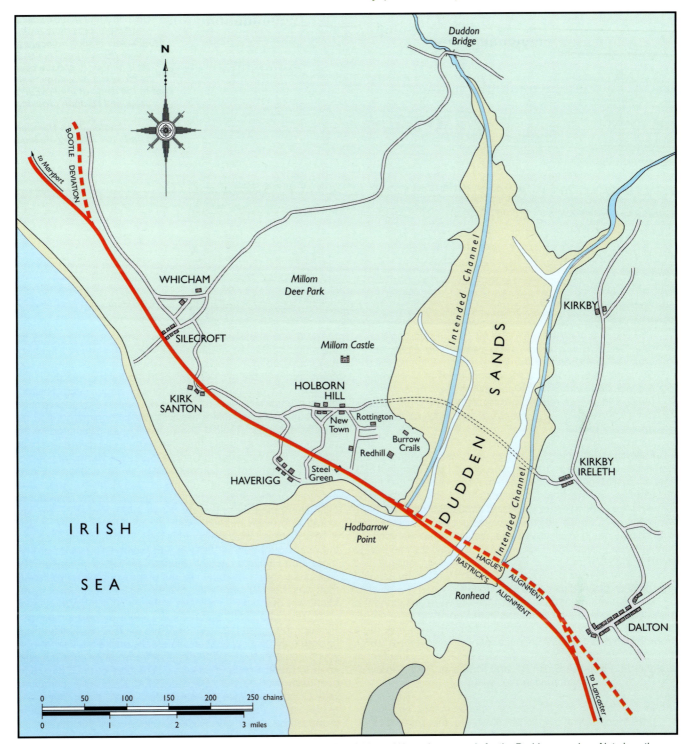

West Cumberland, Furness & Morecambe Bay Railway 1838 Rastrick's and Hague's proposals for the Duddon crossing. Note how the Duddon and Kirkby Pool were to be canalised: the Low Ford route from Holborn Hill to Kirkby Ireleth is also shown.

Drawn by Alan Johnstone, based on a map in the CRA Collection.

The committee seemed to have lost interest in Stephenson's admittedly sketchy plans and on 18th October that same year commissioned John Urpeth Rastrick (1780-1856), an independent civil engineer who had been a judge at the Rainhill Trials and was Engineer of the London & Brighton Railway, to make a detailed survey from Maryport to Lancaster using Hague's line of embankments. Hague's report had already been received but the committee gave instruction that this was not to be made public until Rastrick's report was ready. Reporting back on 24th December, Rastrick revealed that he had surveyed an inland route via Egremont, as well as Stephenson's line via St Bees, before heading south through Ravenglass to Hodbarrow Point. From here the line was to strike directly across the Duddon, south of Stephenson's route, to meet the Lancashire coast at Roanhead, before curving through a deep cutting near Newbiggin and joining Hague's line across Morecambe Bay to Poulton. Like Stephenson, Rastrick did not linger long on the project, spending only a week in the area before leaving his staff to level the various lines. Rastrick's Duddon embankment was higher than Hague's proposal in order to minimise the gradients, there being plenty of material to be excavated from the cuttings required in Furness for this purpose. The Egremont deviation was decided against due to unfavourable gradients and an alternative route passing close to Bootle village did not find favour with its inhabitants. Their descendents, faced with a walk of more than a mile to the eventual station, may have had cause to disagree with their forebears. Rastrick reckoned that the Morecambe Bay embankment would take longer to build than the remainder of the line but he recommended opening the Duddon crossing at the same time as the railway. The *Cumberland Paquet* suggested that the then depressed state of the market and lack of confidence in railway schemes meant that this was not a good time to launch such a scheme but an advertisement in *The Railway Times* of 8th January 1839 for the West Cumberland, Furness & Morecambe Bay Railway confidently read

Chapter Two

On 27th August 1961 Fowler 4F 0-6-0 44347 sits on the Hodbarrow branch adjacent to Millom Ironworks. This SLS/MLS railtour may have been the closest a passenger train got to the route of the W&FJR's proposed Duddon crossing.

Photo: John Marshall/Kidderminster Railway Museum

The Reports of Mr Rastrick and Mr Hague detailing the proposed Railway, which when carried into effect will form the grand connecting line between England and Scotland, through the trading communities of Liverpool, Manchester, and Birmingham, being now before the public and considered highly satisfactory, the promoters have determined to proceed at once to raise the necessary capital.

Following receipt of the Hague and Rastrick reports, the committee took action and gave notice, dated 13th February 1839, that an application was to be made to Parliament in 1840 for an Act to make a railway from Lancaster to Maryport via Morecambe Bay and the Duddon estuary, passing through Millom, Whicham, Whitbeck and Bootle, before traversing other parishes and townships through Whitehaven and Workington to Maryport. A further notice, dated 18th October 1839, detailed the intention to apply in the same or another Act to "embank, drain, enclose and otherwise improve land, sand or soil" within Morecambe Bay and the "estuary, bay or river called the Duddon".

Meanwhile, further east, other interests were agitating for a railway to Scotland over Shap and at this point the government became concerned at the possibility of more than one route from England to Scotland. Consequently, in November 1839, the government appointed two commissioners, Lieutenant Colonel Sir Frederick Smith RE and Professor Peter Barlow of the Royal Military Academy in Woolwich

to enquire and report upon the relative merits, and the preference which might be given, to the respective already-surveyed and projected railways between London and the cities of Edinburgh and Glasgow following, namely via York, Newcastle-upon-Tyne and Berwick, via York, Newcastle-upon-Tyne and Hexham, via Lancaster, Whitehaven and Carlisle and via Lancaster, Penrith and Carlisle; the said enquiry to include the relative merits of the two lines from London to York, by Derby and Rotherham and by Cambridge and Lincoln.

The commissioners produced their report in four parts: the first, in 1840, concerned communication with Dublin; the second, in May 1840, covered the west coast lines to Scotland; part 3, published in November 1840, concerned Grayrigg and the final part, published in March 1841, was about the east coast lines and contained a summary. West Cumberland interests were covered in the second part, where the coastal route was compared with the two versions of the route via Penrith.

The commissioners complimented Hague and Rastrick on their plans and documentation but rejected their proposals on grounds of cost, difficulties with the embankments and the greater distance. Table 1 shows the figures calculated by the commissioners to justify their decision. The average speed figure for the Lancaster to Carlisle journey is worthy of note.

Furthermore, the commissioners were concerned over "numerous discrepancies" in the Hague-Rastrick report over the cost of the embankments, Hague's way of drawing up estimates being described as "loose and uncertain". He was asked to provide more detailed estimates and came up with a 10% increase over his own figures. The report claimed that the cost would be £543,373 2s 11d, some £109,241 14s 7½d more than Hague's original estimate, or a 25% increase! The commissioners came out in favour of the Lune Valley route and thus was West Cumberland's fate sealed by the stroke of a pen. Might the outcome have been different had the Whitehaven committee gone with Stephenson's more modest proposals? Perhaps the coastal route was never a realistic possibility: it was backed only by local business interests, unlike the inland route which could call on outside capital from Lancashire interests keen to reach Scotland this way. The cost of the Shap route eventually worked out at about £21,400 per mile, compared with £22,000 per mile for the modest single track Ulverstone & Lancaster line, with its river crossings shorter than those proposed by Hague and Rastrick. However, it still remains an interesting exercise to speculate on what might have been, and how the prosperity of Millom and other towns in Furness and West Cumberland might have been affected had the West Coast Main Line actually gone around the west coast.

Having lost the argument over the London to Scotland railway, Whitehaven interests turned to something of a more local nature and in February 1842 notice was given that an application was to be made to Parliament in the 1843 session for a railway between Rampside and Maryport. This would pass through Dalton and Ireleth, cross the Duddon sands, pass through Millom, Whicham, Whitbeck and Bootle before continuing via Whitehaven and Workington to terminate by a junction with the Maryport and Carlisle Railway. The M&CR was to open throughout on 10th February 1845.

Table 1 Comparison between the three west coast lines to Scotland			
	Via Coast	Via Kendal	Via Lune Valley
Time, travelling at 22½ mph	4h 23 min	3h 20 min	3h 28 min
Fare Lancaster-Carlisle	15s 9d (79p)	10s 11d (54½p)	11s 7d (58p)
Estimated passengers per annum	8,040	21,528	21,528
Length from Lancaster to Carlisle	94m 45ch	64m 34ch	68m 48ch

The Arrival of the Railway (1835 - 1866)

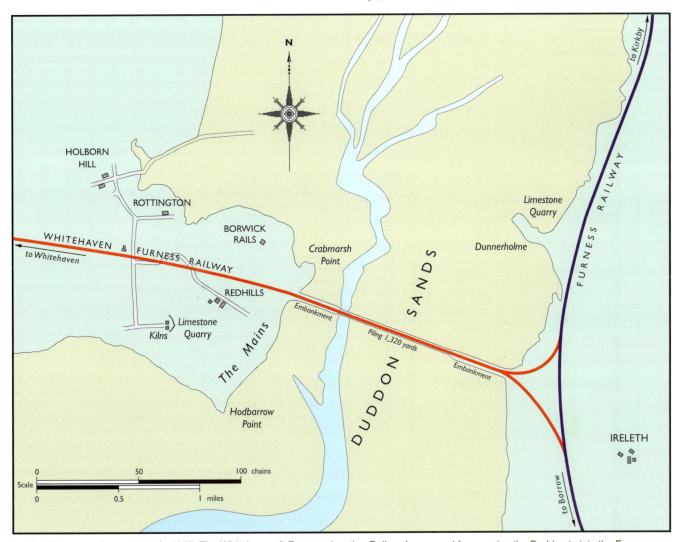

Duddon crossing proposals 1847 The Whitehaven & Furness Junction Railway's proposal for crossing the Duddon to join the Furness Railway. In contemporary documents the full name was often shortened to Whitehaven & Furness Railway.
Drawn by Alan Johnstone, based on a map in the CRA Collection.

In 1843 George Stephenson returned to the scene and, with the eminent civil Engineer Frank Forster (1800-1852), a close friend of George's son Robert since their involvement in building the London & Birmingham Railway in 1830, was commissioned to report on a more modest scheme, the proposed Maryport to Whitehaven line. William, Lord Lowther (1787-1872, later to become Second Earl of Lonsdale following his father's death in March 1844) was behind the drive to establish what was to become the Whitehaven Junction Railway (WJR). The WJR was incorporated on 4th July 1844 with Stephenson as its engineer and was opened for passengers on 19th March 1847, goods traffic having begun on 15th February. Stephenson, through his friendship with the Earl, recommended him to develop the area's mineral wealth by pushing railway construction southwards and Lonsdale responded by setting up yet another committee to promote what would eventually become the Whitehaven & Furness Junction Railway (W&FJR).

The Railway Mania was at its height and the proposed line attracted significant support from Manchester business interests (£111,000) with rather less from London (£2,000) to add to the £10,000 contribution from the Earl himself. Formal notices appeared in November 1844, indicating that it was intended to make an application to Parliament in 1845 to authorise a railway from Whitehaven via St Bees, Sellafield, Drigg, Bootle and Millom, across the Duddon sands and to terminate in a junction with the Furness Railway in "the several townships or divisions of Above Town, Dalton Proper and Yarlside, or some of them, in the Parish of Dalton". Despite the Bill only being to join the FR, grand aspirations still abounded.

The object of the proposed undertaking is the construction of a railway from . . . Whitehaven . . . to join the Furness Railway, . . . now in process of formation, and eventually to extend the same by way of Ulverston to Lancaster. It is proposed to purchase land sufficient for double line and to construct bridges accordingly but until traffic is fully developed to lay down a single line only.

In May 1845 the Tidal Harbours Commission, anxious that the proposed railway might affect shipping in the Duddon estuary, convened an inquest to which George Stephenson was summoned to answer some probing questions. The W&FJR Engineer started by telling the commissioners that the object of the proposals was to "get away the iron-stone; there is a large quantity in that neighbourhood and is sent into various parts of England". The commissioners, concerned about further impact on shipping, asked Stephenson whether part of the plan was to cross Morecambe Bay. He replied that this was not part of the plan but, "we may have another project for Morecambe Bay; there is no plan in Parliament this year but I daresay next year". He was referring to the W&FJR's Lancashire Extension project, of which more later. Responding to further questioning, he stated that the object of crossing the Duddon was to join the Furness & Piel Railway and thence carry traffic from Piel Harbour to the Preston & Wyre Railway. He also expected to carry iron ore from Furness via Whitehaven to Newcastle. The commissioners were concerned over the loss of river access to Broughton-in-Furness but Stephenson assured them that it was intended to give that town a railway which would be at least as beneficial as the existing navigation. The inquest then moved on to the detail of the Duddon crossing and Stephenson outlined his proposal to construct wooden bridges on piles to the height of the intended embankment (some six feet above high water). A steam engine at either side of the estuary would draw wagons across by chain in order to drop out material, over which the water would initially flow. This material would

15

Chapter Two

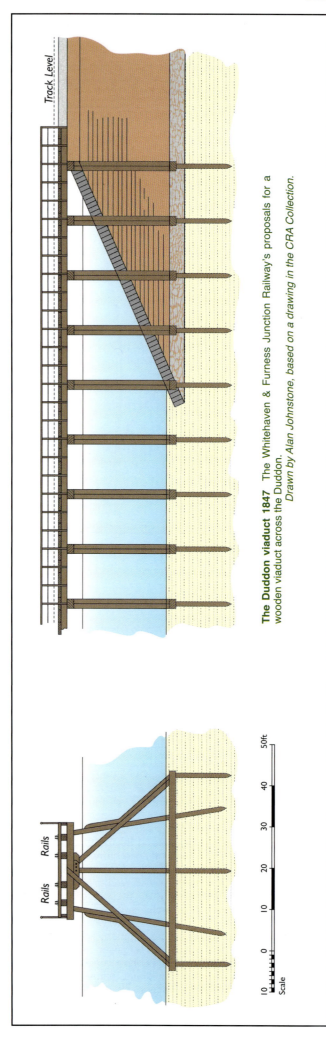

The Duddon viaduct 1847 The Whitehaven & Furness Junction Railway's proposals for a wooden viaduct across the Duddon.
Drawn by Alan Johnstone, based on a drawing in the CRA Collection.

be consolidated from boats and built up until the water did not flow over: the job would be completed by the natural silting of the embankment by sand and a new channel would be cut for the river. Pressing their concerns over potential interruption to navigation, the commissioners suggested the construction of a swing bridge in the embankment but Stephenson was of the view that the current would be too great to allow this. Possibly in desperation, his inquisitors asked if the railway could be taken up the west bank of the river and a crossing made from Shaw Point to Angerton, to which Stephenson predictably pointed out the large detour and said that he would not build such a railway. He didn't, although others eventually would, but by then "Old George" was dead.

Returning to their theme of access to Broughton, the commissioners called Captain Henry Mangles Denham RN and pressed him about the unsuitability of a solid embankment. Unfortunately for their argument, Captain Denham was of the view that so few vessels used the river to carry coal, manure and limestone that it would be more beneficial solid than open, although he did admit that vessels engaged in bringing slate from quarries near Broughton would be cut off. He went on to say that "from the trade I am at all aware of, I imagine it would be very slight privation to the country in general," and informed the commissioners that the estuary was so useless to the Earl of Burlington that he was to "form a railroad".

Despite the responses from Stephenson and Captain Denham, the House of Lords saw fit to amend the W&FJR Bill on 4th July 1845. The Duddon crossing from Crabmarsh to Ireleth was to be an arched embankment or open piling, depending on the Admiralty commissioners' wishes and, following a complaint from "the party at Broughton Tower" that the Duddon was then navigable to within two miles of there, there was to be a swing or draw bridge. The extent of the embankment or piling, span of arches or opening of the piling and the dimensions and site of the bridge were to be determined by the Admiralty commissioners. Furthermore, the railway company would be fined £10 if it was responsible for any vessels being detained while navigating the river, and was required to deepen, straighten and secure by sea walls the main stream above and below the embankment so that navigation of the Duddon was not interrupted. The W&FJR Bill received the Royal Assent on 21st July 1845 but, in November before construction of the railway had even started, the directors gave notice that plans were to be put before Parliament in the following year to connect with the WJR via a tunnel and to vary the route between Whicham and Chapel Sucken for a length of two miles and 58 chains. The Act for these changes, passed on 3rd August 1846, gave additional powers to raise £25,000 by shares and to borrow £8,333 in addition to £350,000 in shares and £116,600 borrowing authorised by the 1845 Act. The company was still determined to get its Lancashire Extension from Ulverston to Carnforth through Parliament and claimed to have made arrangements to join the North Western Railway at Carnforth. Shareholders wanted none of this and complained that the funds they had provided were being diverted away from the building of the line agreed in the Act. The Lancashire Extension Bill came before Parliament in the 1846 Session but was strongly opposed by local landowners and was rejected by the Standing Order Committee, leaving the W&FJR belatedly to turn its attentions back to its line down the Cumbrian coast and across the Duddon. However the concept of a railway from Whitehaven to Carnforth did not go away immediately and Lonsdale was still informing the W&FJR directors in February 1851 that a Bill for such a line was to be brought before Parliament in the 1852 session. The *Railway Record* commented in March 1852 that the view was rapidly gaining ground that the W&FJR would ultimately cross the bay to Lancaster.

In late 1846, construction of the W&FJR eventually got under way from the Whitehaven end, with James Dees (1815-1875) as Engineer and Messrs Fell & Joplin and Brotherton & Rigg as the main contracting partnerships. Dees was prominent in Cumbrian railway engineering around this time, having moved to Cumberland in 1845 as Assistant Resident Engineer of the W&FJR under Stephenson. He served as Engineer to the Maryport & Carlisle (1850-59), the WJR up to 1856 and the Whitehaven, Cleator & Egremont from 1854 to 1857. He was also manager of the W&FJR and a director of

The Arrival of the Railway (1835 - 1866)

On 4th July 1955, Ivatt Class 4MT 43006 is seen hauling the Class J 2-30pm Mineral from Egremont to Millom through the cutting near Oxenbows Farm. When the railway was being built around 1850 the contractors engaged in digging the cutting stabled their horses at the nearby Drinkells (Drinkalds) Farm. Haverigg crossing can be glimpsed in the distance and Langthwaite Farm is on the skyline.
Photo: CRA Library Ref PEJ158

the Cockermouth & Workington and Solway Junction Railways. Before the end of that first year, the W&FJR's directors were again giving notice of changes. The Railway Mania was over and would-be speculators had realised that railways were not as lucrative as they had been led to believe, leaving the W&FJR short of capital. This resulted in a major change of heart over the Duddon crossing and, having failed to convince the inhabitants of Broughton to allow the cheaper option of a Duddon crossing without the swing bridge specified in the Act, in November 1847 notice was given that an approach was to be made to Parliament in the following year to abandon the line between Silecroft and the FR at Ireleth. Instead, an extension or deviation line from Silecroft would be constructed and a junction made with the FR Broughton extension at Foxfield. At the W&FJR's first half-yearly meeting in 1848, the chairman, the Earl of Lonsdale, pointed out the advantages of the Deviation Bill then before Parliament: the original three mile viaduct would be replaced by a structure of only one mile, located some four miles upstream, and there would be no need to construct a swing bridge. Underlining the new railway's financial difficulties, it was reported that the revised crossing would save some £35,000 and that the company's arrears amounted to some £33,200, necessitating "more stringent measures to be adopted to enforce the payment of calls". Given the previous antagonism towards the original crossing by the Lords and the Tidal Harbours Commission, it is hardly surprising that the Admiralty gave their full assent to the revised crossing of the river, stating on 28th March 1848 that it was better in every way than the original. They noted that the village of Broughton was above the bridge but no vessels went there; however they required that provision should be made in the Bill for the establishment of an opening bridge in case their Lordships were to deem it desirable in the future. Lonsdale must have been disappointed to learn that a moveable bridge might still be required although, in the event, it was never built. The new line with its less impressive viaduct was authorised by the W&FJR Amendment Act of 14th August, which required no additional capital, and by the time of the second half-yearly meeting held later that same month the chairman was sufficiently confident to report that it was now hoped to save £37,000 by bridging the Duddon where it was only ¼ mile wide instead of the planned 1½ mile crossing. The distances seemed to vary somewhat!

Construction of the railway from Whitehaven appears to have been without major problems and the first 16¼ miles of the line from Preston Street to Ravenglass were opened on 19th July 1849, with a connecting 17 mile coach journey by road to Broughton-in-Furness. The directors were obviously anxious to attract as much business as possible and the *Ulverston Advertiser* of 17th January 1850 advised that general merchandise and small parcels could be delivered at Gosforth, Holmrook and all places on the road between Ravenglass and Broughton, Dalton and Ulverston. The prices, which varied from 3d to 15½d (1p to 6½p) per hundredweight and between 3d and 18d (1p and 7½p) for parcels, dependent on distance and weight of parcel, included collection and delivery. The next 4¾ miles of railway to Bootle were inspected by Captain G Wynne RE and in his first report, dated 9th June 1850, he considered the girders of the under-bridge immediately north of the Esk viaduct to be of insufficient strength and the track layout at Bootle to be unsafe. To add to the W&FJR's woes, the Esk viaduct caught fire during the early hours of 28th June and about 60 yards of the structure was destroyed at its southern end but frantic activity by the workmen enabled the damaged timber to be completely replaced by 1st July. Little more than six years later W&FJR guards reported the viaduct as unsafe. Were the 1850 repairs too hurried?

Following the installation of new girders on the under-bridge and a revised track arrangement at Bootle, Captain Wynne re-inspected the line and it was opened to the public on 8th July, with a coach again providing onward connections to Broughton. The *Ulverston Advertiser* reported on 3rd October 1850 that

17

Chapter Two

DUDDON SANDS VIADUCT.

This view of the W&FJR's viaduct across the Duddon at Foxfield shows the first passenger train heading towards Broughton in 1850. This single track wooden structure, a far cry from the grand schemes planned to cross the mouth of the estuary, was referred to as 'The Spile Bridge'.
Photo: CRA Library Ref MO0871

"on Tuesday last [1st October], Messrs Fell and Jopling took an engine through their contract from Foxfield, near Broughton, where the Whitehaven line joins the Furness line, to Sylecroft [sic], the end of their contract." Brotherton and Rigg sold their plant at Sykebeck, south of Bootle on 5th February 1851, on which occasion the unfortunate guard of the 10-15am train from Whitehaven lost his life when he came into contact with an overbridge as he climbed over the top of a carriage to apply the brake for the special Sykebeck stop. In contrast, the sale of Fell and Jopling's plant at Foxfield did not occur until 1st September 1852, nearly two years after the railway had opened. The final section from Bootle to Broughton was passed by the Board of Trade inspector, Lieutenant Galton, on 24th October 1850 and the single track line officially opened on 29th October, albeit somewhat later than the directors had hoped and more than five years after the W&FJR's original Act had been given the Royal Assent. It was far removed from the grandiose double-track main line originally envisaged and was described by Marshall and Walton as "a cheap and ill-tracked line down the south west Cumberland coast". The *Whitehaven Herald* of 2nd November 1850 described the celebrations at the official opening of the line, when a "select party of some sixty gentlemen" and the Earl of Lonsdale set off from the Newtown Station, Whitehaven to arrive at Broughton-in-Furness about an hour and half later. The *Illustrated London News* of 9th November went on to say

The whole population of the place seemed astir, with a view to giving écla to the ceremony. They were accompanied by a band of music and flag-bearers; and the airs they played, if not classical, were at least

The Hodbarrow branch curves away towards the ironworks behind the gas holder in this view showing Stanier Class 5MT 45402 on 19th July 1961. The site of the original level crossing is at the end of the Down platform just beyond the second LMS 'Hawkseye' name board. Some of the last houses built in Newtown in Market Street and Lonsdale Road are seen beyond the coal yard on former FR land.
Photo: CRA Library Ref PES366

The Arrival of the Railway (1835 - 1866)

enlivening and appropriate. A very tasteful triumphal arch had been erected in front of the station, composed of evergreens and garlands, and the road leading from the station to the Old King's Head, where an excellent dinner had been prepared, was also decorated with such flowers and plants as the season could afford.

Shortly after the arrival of the Whitehaven train, the FR train from Furness Abbey arrived bearing the Earl of Burlington and other gentlemen. At the dinner, the Earl of Lonsdale spoke with optimism about the future and of the other lines expected to join theirs, particularly from the Coniston copper mines and from Ulverston across Morecambe Bay to the Lancaster & Carlisle line.

The full line opened to the public on 1st November. Intermediate stations were St Bees (4 miles from Whitehaven), Nethertown (7 miles), Braystones (8½ miles), Sellafield (10½ miles), Seascale (12½ miles), Drigg (14½ miles), Ravenglass (16½ miles), Eskmeals (18 miles), Bootle (21 miles), Silecroft (26 miles), Holborn Hill (29½ miles) and Underhill (31 miles) with Green Road (32 miles) formally opening in 1853. The last station appears as a footnote in the timetable of 1st November 1850 as "Nos. 1 and 3 Up and Down trains will stop to take up and set down Passenger, Parcels and Light Goods at the Green Road, in Millom, when required to do so". Whitbeck Crossing and Kirksanton Crossing first appeared in the timetable in July 1854. According to John Linton, writing in 1852, "at about three miles from Bootle the engine generally stops to take in water, and here we shall have time to take a leisurely view of the village and church of Whitbeck". Neither Whitbeck nor Kirksanton lasted very long, both featuring in the timetables for the last time in September 1857, the latter station reportedly opening only on market day. By around 1860, with the exception of Bootle, the stations between the Esk and the Duddon all had similar track layouts. Eskmeals, at the south end of the 319 yard long timber Esk viaduct with its 36 openings, had a single siding leading to a coal depot; Bootle, as befitted the principal settlement in the area, had the most extensive facilities, boasting a passing loop, two-road coal depot and additional sidings; Silecroft had a passing loop and two sidings, one serving a coal depot; Holborn Hill had a passing loop and a single siding; Underhill had a passing loop and two sidings, one serving a coal depot, and Green Road had only a single siding. All the stations, except Eskmeals where the road crossed under the railway at the end of the viaduct, were situated at the level intersection of the railway with a public road and, in the cases where a passing loop was provided, the level crossing was on the double track section. The roads crossing the railway at Holborn Hill, Underhill and Green Road all led to fords across the Duddon. Holborn Hill station was situated to the north-east of the current Furness Railway-built Millom station and, since the building of the railway had severed the original road leading through Holborn Hill village to the Duddon sands, access to the ford was gained indirectly from a junction with the old road leading from Salthouse to Lapstone Lodge immediately south of the railway level crossing. The typical W&FJR station comprised a wooden office, some ten feet square, and an open-fronted wooden shelter 12ft by 8ft. The platform surfaces were in need of attention by 1861 when the Board agreed to make them good with gravel and ballast, having dismissed the superior alternatives of stone flags, bricks or asphalt. Looking back 50 years in 1916, the *Millom Gazette* noted "The local station itself must have been somewhat of an eyesore for it is recorded that a large old box comprised the passengers' platform, whilst an old worn-out railway guard's van stood for use as a goods station". However, the W&FJR Board had sanctioned the construction of gentlemen's facilities in March 1859. At its meeting on 26th October 1857 the Board agreed to a request for a pay rise from Mr J Hellon, the Holborn Hill Station Master; in recognition of "his efficient services both as regards working the telegraph and constant attendance" he was henceforth to receive £1 a week. In contrast, the new St Bees Station Master, appointed at this time, would receive £60 per annum. Hellon was to stay in post at Holborn Hill until at least 1865, when he was suspended due to a shortage in his takings. He subsequently paid up and was reinstated.

Although, as mentioned in Chapter 1, the W&FJR opened a new wharf at Underhill in 1854 to deal with mineral traffic from the mines in the vicinity, passenger traffic at Underhill and Green Road failed to live up to expectations. In November 1859 the W&FJR Board decided to close these two stations to passengers from 1st January 1860 but, following the announcement of their intentions, a memorial (petition) requesting that Green Road be kept open, and signed by 206 persons, was received. The directors relented and the station stayed open but Underhill was closed as intended. In February 1860 a similar memorial was received from the inhabitants of Millom and neighbourhood in respect of Underhill but the Board would not accede to this and the station remained closed.

The viaduct over the Duddon at Foxfield, known locally as the "Spile Bridge", (a spile is a post used as a foundation) was 592 yards long and consisted of some 50 spans resting on open timber piling accommodating a single line of rails about eight feet above the high water mark for spring tides. The 1845 Act had specified a south-facing junction with the Furness Railway at Foxfield but instead the line as built turned north-east shortly after crossing the Duddon and joined the FR Broughton extension, opened in February 1848, in a direction towards that town. The station at Broughton (35 miles from Whitehaven) was shared with the FR, the W&FJR paying the FR an annual toll of £150 for access. The present line from the east end of the viaduct to Foxfield station (referred to as the *Reverse Curve* by the W&FJR directors and as the *Expedition Curve* by the FR) was not opened until 1st August 1858.

The timetable for the newly-opened line shows that not only were there very few trains (only three each way on weekdays) but also that up to three hours was required for the journey between Whitehaven and Broughton. Apart from the low speeds

Green Road station looking towards Millom in the mid-1930s. The FR Up Starter, operated by lever No 3, still has its pulley and rungs but, in addition, has acquired a ladder. The W&FJR station was on the same site and the road to the High Ford across the Duddon crossed the railway here.

Photo: CRA Library Ref PA0134

Chapter Two

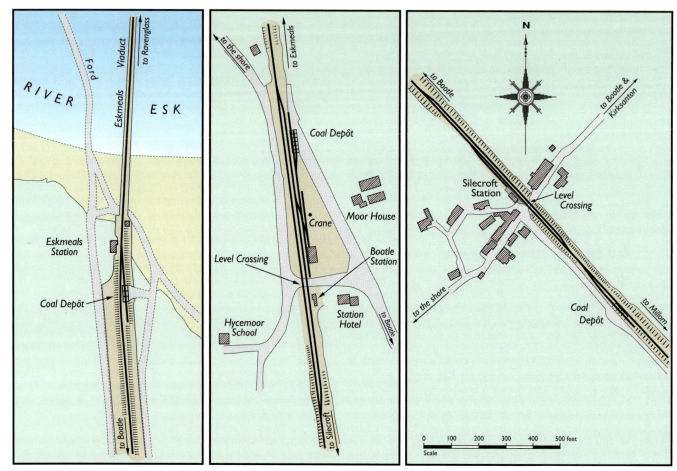

Left: Eskmeals Station circa 1860 The original W&FJR station at the southern end of the Esk viaduct. **Centre: Bootle Station circa 1860** This was the principal settlement between the Esk and the Duddon and had the most extensive facilities of all the W&FJR stations on this section. **Right: Silecroft Station circa 1860** The street layout of Silecroft is little changed over 150 years later.

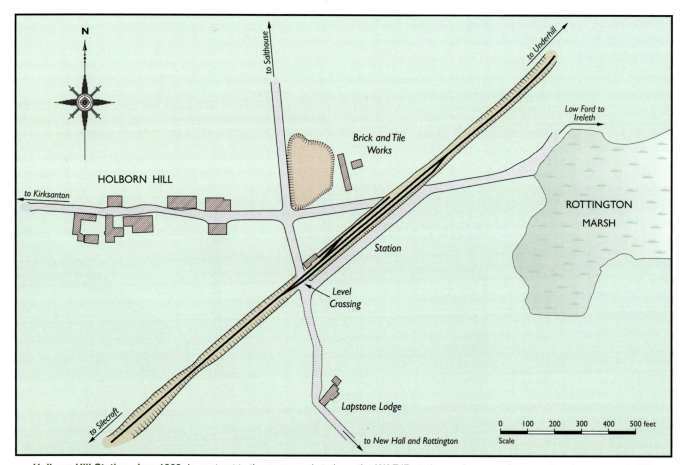

Holborn Hill Station circa 1860 In contrast to the more rural stations, the W&FJR station and surroundings are largely unrecognisable today. The present Millom station lies immediately to the south west of the level crossing. Notice how the railway has severed the original road from Holborn Hill to the Low Ford.

The Arrival of the Railway (1835 - 1866)

Underhill Station circa 1860
Underhill, unlike Holborn Hill, warranted a coal depôt, on the site of which Underhill Cottages were built around 1890.

Station plans drawn by Alan Johnstone and are based on maps in the CRA Collection.

Green Road Station circa 1860 Like Holborn Hill and Underhill, Green Road was sited where the road to the Duddon ford crossed the line.

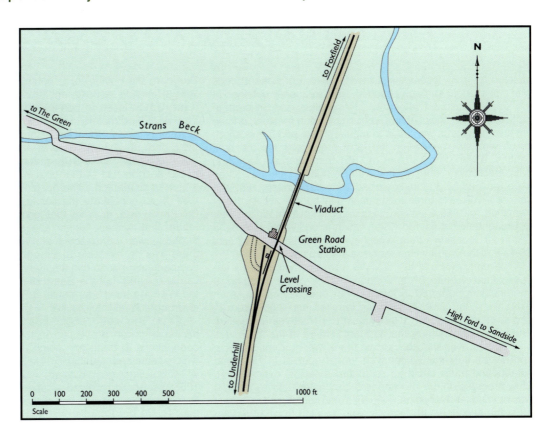

Chapter Two

CRA Collection.

attained by early locomotives, trains, which were often goods with a passenger carriage attached, were frequently detained at the smaller stations (Nethertown, Ravenglass and Silecroft, in particular) while cock fighting went on. Station masters, engine drivers and guards were said to regularly take part in this sport, which was still reported in the local press well into the next century. During the summer of 1851 there was an additional train each way and Whitehaven-Broughton journey times were reduced by 30 minutes or so: from 1st January 1852 the service reverted to three trains each way but the accelerations remained. In 1850 a second class single ticket from Whitehaven to Broughton cost 5s 10d (29p), which is equivalent to around £23 in 2012; a single from Whitehaven to Foxfield in 2012 cost £8.40 and the journey time was less than an hour.

The early years of the W&FJR were characterised by the unsatisfactory state of its finances: many of the company's shareholders preferred to forfeit rather than pay calls. As an example, 4,000 shares had been forfeited and 2,000 were in course of being forfeited at the August 1849 half-yearly meeting. The mineral traffic over the northern portion of the route was only carried over short distances; there was no through traffic northwards until the Whitehaven tunnel opened in 1852 and southbound traffic could go no further than Piel over the FR. Slow progress on the Ulverstone & Lancaster Railway (U&LR) was blamed for the company's poor traffic figures and in August 1854 the secretary, JS Yeats Jr, was directed to write to John Brogden, the driving force behind the U&LR, saying that the W&FJR would oppose any fresh application to Parliament if the U&LR failed to complete its line in the time specified. The W&FJR directors were overjoyed when the railway from Ulverston to Carnforth finally opened on 26th August 1857: they had at last obtained a route south for Cumberland haematite, coal and iron to reach the rest of the country and in the second half of that year a first dividend, albeit a lowly 1%, was distributed. The opening of the U&LR prompted the W&FJR to accelerate the services between Whitehaven and Broughton and, in order that locomotives did not have to run tender first at these higher speeds (35-40 miles per hour), a turntable was constructed at Whitehaven (Bransty). Since there was no turntable at Broughton, it is presumed that the company planned to use the triangle formed when the Reverse Curve opened, but the Board of Trade subsequently required the W&FJ to build a turntable at Foxfield and the original route to Broughton fell into disuse.

From the late 1850s onwards, the rise of haematite mining and iron production in the district and the enhanced connections to north and south (but not passenger numbers, which remained stubbornly low) dramatically improved the W&FJR's financial situation. Consequently, in September 1863 the Board received a report from its Engineer, Thomas Drane, on the cost of a line across the Duddon estuary to join the FR. At the Board's next meeting the following month the

The Arrival of the Railway (1835 - 1866)

The Hodbarrow branch is pictured looking towards the ironworks on 19th July 1961. The W&FJR's line across the Duddon would have left the Hodbarrow branch just behind the photographer and headed across the sands behind the ground frame hut on the left.

Photo: CRA Library Ref PES363

Duddon crossing was again considered but it was felt that traffic prospects were insufficiently encouraging to warrant re-applying to Parliament for powers in the 1864 session. However by the autumn of 1864, the directors' confidence had been restored. The Earl of Lonsdale told shareholders at the half-yearly meeting in September that "the line passed through a thinly populated district but the iron ore had been their friend" and at the Board meeting on 10th October it was agreed to engage James Brunlees to report on the practicability and probable cost of a line across the Duddon to join the FR. From a financial viewpoint, this was a justifiable decision. Table 2 shows the improving state of the company's finances; the 1863-6 average dividend compares very well with that of all British railway companies over the same period, which stood at only 4%. Due largely to the national demand for haematite, the West Cumberland lines at the time showed dividends unequalled anywhere in the country, with the Furness Railway average over the years 1863-66 being an equally healthy 9½%. Additionally, it had not escaped the W&FJR directors' notice that the output from the Hodbarrow mine was escalating rapidly and that most of it was leaving the area by sea: production from Hodbarrow was 32,521 tons in 1863, 78,993 tons in 1864

Table 2 *Whitehaven & Furness Junction Railway and Furness Railway yearly dividends*

	1858	1859	1860	1861	1862	1863	1864	1863-6 *
W&FJR	1¼	2½	3½	3⅛	2¾	5¼	5¾	9½
FR	6½	6½	7½	8	8	8½	10	9½

*Average figure

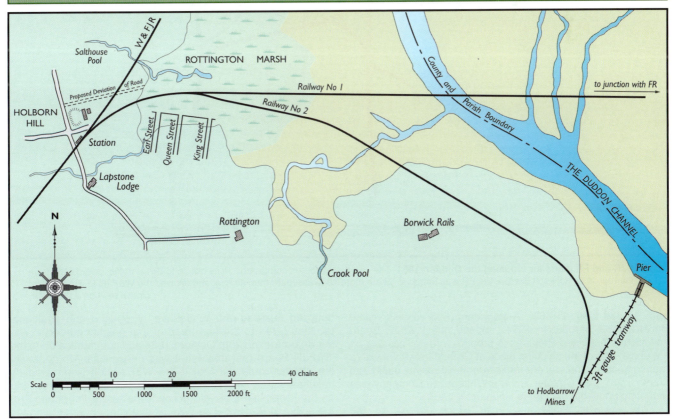

Duddon Crossing 1864 This was the W&FJR's second attempt at crossing the Duddon. Railway No 2 was the only portion built and note how its embankment provided reclaimed land to build the new town.

Drawn by Alan Johnstone, based on a map in the CRA Collection.

Chapter Two

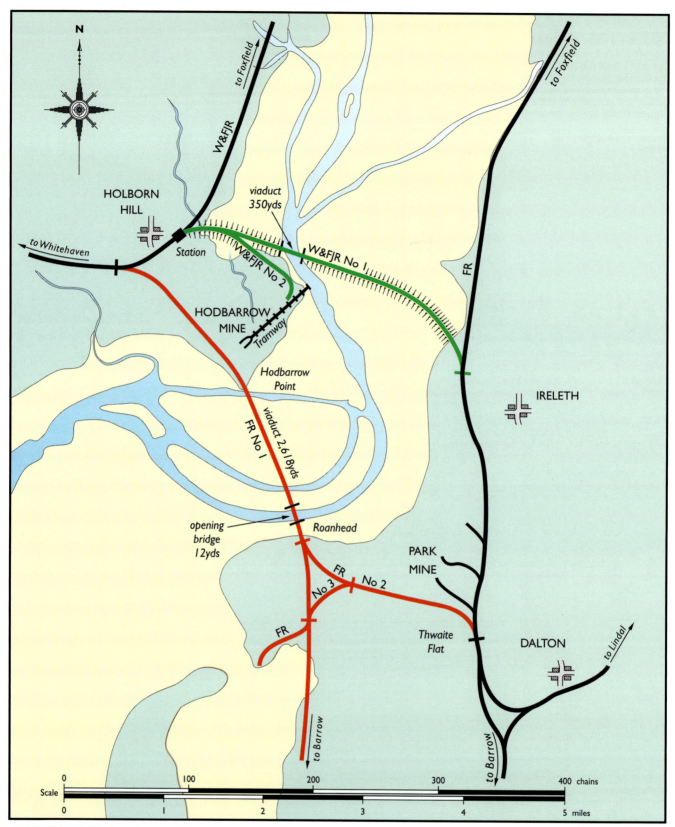

W&FJR and FR plans for crossing the Duddon 1864 The competing routes compared. In its desire to divert traffic, particularly from Hodbarrow, to its docks at Barrow, the FR was forced to take a more seaward route than its rival and allowed the W&FJR to win the day.
Drawn by Alan Johnstone.

and 117,329 tons in 1865. A staggering 600 vessels visited Borwick Rails harbour in 1864. Indeed, the W&FJR Board specifically instructed Brunlees to prepare a route "passing on the upper side of the shipping place at Crab Marsh Point with a branch to obtain the iron ore traffic from the tramway near Crab Marsh Point" (see Chapter 3). The Whitehaven Company was mounting an all-out bid for the Hodbarrow traffic.

The *Railway News and Joint Stock Journal* of 8th September 1864 considered that the Duddon crossing scheme had much to recommend it since "several miles in distance would be saved, large quantities of land reclaimed, trains between Furness and Whitehaven expedited and additional facilities given to the iron trade of that neighbourhood". The FR Board met on 28th October 1864 and communicated to the W&FJR Board that they felt it was unnecessary to construct the shorter route but that if the W&FJR felt it immediately necessary then the FR would be willing to co-operate so long as the proposals took into account the "great importance" of the docks at Barrow. The W&FJR directors agreed to join the FR in shortening the route by a new line from Holborn Hill to Lindal if the latter company would apply for powers from the point of junction to Lindal but that if the FR were to decline the

The Arrival of the Railway (1835 - 1866)

Hodbarrow pier looking north-west. The ironworks is seen in the distance beyond Borwick Rails harbour and Duddon Villa can be glimpsed behind the Hunslet 0-4-0ST. The paddle tug Duddon is sitting in the Duddon channel. The volume of shipping from this pier was one of the reasons that the Furness Railway's plans for the Duddon crossing were dismissed in favour of the Whitehaven & Furness Junction proposals.
Photo: Peter Holmes Collection

proposal then the W&FJR would cross the Duddon themselves "at such point as they deem expedient". Powers for crossing the estuary had been included in the W&FJR Act of 1845 but had since lapsed and so the Whitehaven directors gave notice of their intentions to apply to Parliament for an Act in the 1865 session. The proposal was to construct a double track railway (Number 1) from immediately on the north-eastern side of the road which crossed the railway adjacent to the booking office at Holborn Hill station, thence across the Duddon sands to terminate by a junction with the FR 600 yards north of the point where the road from Ireleth to Duddon sands crossed that railway. The viaduct spanning the Duddon channel would be 350 yards long, comprising 35 spans of 30ft each and the total length of this proposed railway would be 3 miles, 2 furlongs and 3 chains. Also to be included in the Bill was a branch line (Number 2) off Railway Number 1, commencing 950 yards east from the booking office at Holborn Hill and terminating in a close belonging to the Earl of Lonsdale 300 yards south-west of the end of the pier owned by the Hodbarrow Mining Company at Crab Marsh Point, adjacent to the latter's tramway. All this would require additional capital of £120,000 and a £40,000 loan (around £15 million at 2012 prices).

Unsurprisingly, the FR Board declined to support the W&FJR scheme which would have bypassed its rapidly growing (and increasingly expensive) docks at Barrow and wrote to the Whitehaven company's directors on 3rd November 1864 indicating their intention to deposit their own Bill for a line across the Duddon. Their Railway Number 1 would start in the township of Hawcoat by a junction with the Hawcoat branch and terminate in the township of Millom Below by a junction with the W&FJR 233 yards east along the line from milepost 29 (miles from Whitehaven). Railways 2 and 3 would form a triangular junction with Railway Number 1 and join the FR line to Kirkby at Thwaite Flat. Both the W&FJR and FR Bills were to be laid before Parliament in the 1865 session but, whereas the FR invited the W&FJR to hold shares in the new railway and to enter into agreements over the working, use, management, maintenance and supply of rolling stock and staff via a Joint Committee, the W&FJR made no mention of the FR in their notice. The W&FJR directors "regretted to find that the Furness Company, with whom we have hitherto been in amicable relationships, have also deposited a Bill for the same purpose, thus proposing to invade the territory which legitimately belongs to this Company." The scene was again set for more lengthy (and expensive) arguments over the Duddon crossing.

Before the issue had had time to come before the Parliamentary committee, the *Railway News and Joint Stock Journal* of 11th February 1865 reported on the competing schemes, the FR's with John McClean and Frank Stileman as engineers and the W&FJR with James Brunlees. The *Journal* thought the FR scheme convenient for the south of the Furness peninsula but disadvantaged by its £165,000 cost and 9½ mile length, while the W&FJR proposal was less exposed to the sea, was in shallower water, caused no obstruction to shipping, was cheaper at £65,000, was only 3¼ miles long and "accommodates an important station at Holborn Hill". Whilst obviously favouring the Whitehaven company's proposals, the *Journal* went on, "we cannot but think both of these schemes partial and imperfect as they stand". It is interesting to note that two months previously the same journal was of the view that "the Furness as the more enterprising and popular company will receive the most support and is likely to be successful".

The two schemes came before a Parliamentary committee on 13th March 1865, where the arguments, and ultimately the outcome, centred around the rapidly developing Hodbarrow mine. Speaking for the FR, the hugely influential Henry Schneider MP (see Chapter 1) felt that the iron ore from Hodbarrow should be taken to Barrow for shipment in order to avoid the dangerous harbour of Borwick Rails, thereby negating the advantages claimed by the W&FJR of not interfering with navigation to and from the harbour. In reply, the Hodbarrow company claimed that if they relied on shipping their ore through Barrow, costs would rise by a shilling (5p) per ton because of the extra rail mileage and payment of Barrow harbour dues. In its report, published on 13th June that year, the committee noted that the W&FJR scheme interfered with access to the smaller navigation above the Borwick Rails harbour, but was much more concerned over the FR's long (2,618 yards) single track viaduct that interfered with access to the harbour itself. However, the main objection was to the proposed 36ft wide opening span in the FR scheme, which the committee felt was too narrow and exposed for "the large and increasing trade with the harbour" and the W&FJR proposals received Parliamentary support. The Act approving the W&FJR's Duddon crossing and the Hodbarrow branch received the Royal Assent on 29th June 1865.

On 7th July 2012 Metro-Cammell-built unit 156 479 passes under Moor Bridge, Millom on its way to Carlisle, where it will arrive some two hours later. It is rounding the sharp curve authorised by the W&FJR Amendment Act of 1848 and is soon to join the original alignment authorised by the 1845 Act.
Photo: Alan Johnstone

Following the committee's decision and before the Act was passed, the FR quickly offered terms for amalgamation. The two chairmen had met in May to set up an agreement for the FR to lease the W&FJR and guaranteeing Whitehaven shareholders 8% on Ordinary Capital, although informed opinion on the FR Board was that Lonsdale would not lease the W&FJR without the WJR. Both boards met during late May and early June and a special meeting of W&FJR shareholders was convened on 26th June, with the result that an agreement was reached for the FR to lease the Whitehaven company from 1st July 1865. Although the Furness Board was advised to purchase the WJR, the London & North Western Railway seized the initiative and absorbed it, together with the Cockermouth & Workington Railway, on 16th July 1866.

The end of the W&FJR as a separate company was now in sight but there was still the business of the Hodbarrow branch to resolve. The Hodbarrow Mining Company wrote to the Board in July objecting to the proposed route of the branch and the directors agreed to vary the route accordingly. This acquiescence was hardly surprising since the arguments surrounding the mine's output had underpinned much of the Parliamentary committee debate and, significantly, Hodbarrow's Nathaniel Caine (of whom more in Chapter 3) wrote to the W&FJR Board in November 1865 protesting that the witnesses he had procured to speak against the FR Bill for the Duddon crossing had not yet been paid. The tender from Messrs T&J Hunter of Barrow for £5,725 was the lowest of the three opened at the Board meeting on 3rd September 1865 and was duly accepted. When Hunter wrote to the W&FJR Board admitting his company's tender was £342 in error, the directors resolved, at their October meeting, to refer the matter to the FR and only to agree to the request if that company gave its consent: the FR was now firmly in charge. Land purchases for the branch commenced at the end of 1865.

Whether Lonsdale had used the whole episode to ensure co-operation between the two companies or even to force the FR to buy the Whitehaven company at a good price, the Furness had been out-manoeuvred and at the W&FJR half yearly meeting held on 15th February 1866 the chairman, Mr W Furness, remarked that "they were now working the line for another company and receiving 8%, a bargain with which he expressed himself well pleased". The Bill came before Parliament in February 1866 "to affect the amalgamation from 1st July 1865 by dissolving the W&FJR and vesting the undertaking in the FR"; it was unopposed and, more than a year after the event, the Furness Railway (Whitehaven Amalgamation) Act received the Royal Assent on 16th July 1866. The LNWR Act to take over the WJR was passed on the same day. At this time *The Railway News* described the local railways as "an extraordinary network of comparatively small lines between Morecambe Bay and Solway Firth . . . by far the most prosperous in the kingdom". Notwithstanding the bourgeoning iron ore traffic from West Cumberland and Hodbarrow, local opinion was that the Furness had paid very dearly for their acquisition and, as events were to prove, they would need to invest heavily in their new line.

William, Second Earl of Lonsdale, only lived a further six years after the FR takeover of "his" line, his major investment in the W&FJR having given him very little return over the years. The Earl was not always well regarded by the local press, but the *Whitehaven News*, reporting on 7th March 1872, honoured him as "the mainspring and mainstay of the coast lines of railway."

The Furness Railway's activities between the Esk and the Duddon continue in Chapter 6 but for now the narrative must return to the 1850s to continue the saga of prospecting for haematite, the mineral on which the town of Millom's very existence depended.

Hodbarrow - a Great Mine (1855-1968)

Birth of a mine; maritime activity; railway developments; the sea walls; twentieth century conflicts; the long decline.

3

"Millom is a town but for an accident of nature would have never become involved in any other industry than tourism."   Investors Chronicle

MENTION OF the Earls of Lonsdale has already been made in Chapter 2. With Hodbarrow the family, which owned huge tracts of Cumberland and Westmorland, was again to have a major influence on the fortunes of south-west Cumberland. As early as 1843 William Lowther, First Earl of Lonsdale, in connection with Messrs Taylor of London, had incurred large losses in searching for iron ore in the carboniferous limestone at Towsey Hole, near Hodbarrow Point. Here the veins of haematite could be seen on the shores of the Duddon estuary. James Davis, already mentioned in Chapter 1, tried his luck at Hodbarrow but it was not until the granting of a take note (lease) by the Second Earl to two men in 1855 that the story of a mine which would change the face of this remote corner of Cumberland really began. Nathaniel Caine (1808-1877) was an iron merchant and philanthropist from Liverpool and John Barratt (1793-1866) was a mine captain from Cornwall who had migrated, via the Duke of Devonshire's lead mines at Grassington, to manage the Coniston copper mines. Arriving around 1830, Barratt had succeeded well at Coniston and lived in some style at *Holywath*. The house was later occupied, until his death in 2009, by Major John Hext, the railway enthusiast and miniature railway owner whose family was related by marriage to the Barratts. Caine became involved after having had dinner with a friend in Ulverston who had lent money to Barratt in an unsuccessful search for iron ore. Rather than lend more money, Caine advised setting up a company with Barratt, himself and his friend – surely, a life-changing decision. Caine maintained his Liverpool connections, spending the summers at his home, *Broomhill,* at Broughton-in-Furness and the rest of the year in Liverpool, where he was a county magistrate. He left £600,000 on his death (equivalent to around £30 million today), the bulk of which was gained through his success at Hodbarrow.

Using the Barratt family capital (in 1863 the Barratt family owned 59 out of the 100 company shares, 52 of them in the hands of John himself) and driven by Caine's energy and perseverance, the company gradually took shape between 1856 and 1860. Beside these two, the original group of shareholders included William Barratt (John's cousin), Dr Robert Turner Bywater of Coniston, William Sproston Caine (Nathaniel's brother), James Barratt (John's brother?), John Bewley (a Liverpool accountant) and Thomas Woodburne (an Ulverston solicitor and probably the friend of Caine referred to in the previous paragraph). Moreover, Barratt and Caine were not content with this single venture; in October 1863 they formed the Ireleth Mining Company with Bewley to search for ore on the Lancashire side of the Duddon and in 1864 they were involved with the Millom Mining Company near The Hill. Unlike Hodbarrow, neither of these ventures yielded a profit on their investment.

The Law Times of 14th July 1855 advertised that the Steel Green Estate was available and observed that "in the hands of an enterprising capitalist the estate might prove a lucrative investment by being converted into a public sea-bathing resort or as a private marine residence". No mention

John Barratt (1793-1866) had successfully mined for copper in Cornwall, lead in Yorkshire and copper at Coniston before arriving at Hodbarrow to search for iron in 1854. The Barratt family provided much of the capital and mining knowledge that enabled the Hodbarrow venture to succeed.
Photo: Millom Discovery Centre Collection

Nathaniel Caine (1808-1877) was a partner in a Liverpool firm of iron merchants and it was his energy that turned the Hodbarrow venture into such a profitable business. He was described as "forceful and pushing with a touch of brusqueness".
Photo: Millom Discovery Centre Collection

Chapter Three

Where the whole story began. Engine shaft was begun in 1855 during the first year of the Hodbarrow partnership and a payment of £206 was made towards the cost of the steam engine there in 1856. The limestone construction of the engine house is typical of the earliest buildings at the Old Mine, although some of the surface installations were temporary structures that could be dismantled or abandoned easily.

Photo: Stephe Cove Collection

was made of the possibility of iron ore beneath the property but "enterprising capitalist" John Barratt obviously realised that this was at least a possibility and bought the property, which eventually passed to the mining company in 1870. In 1856 the prospectors reached "about 80ft of solid haematite" and eventually revealed a body of ore that was the largest in England and the biggest in the world until the opening of the Lake Superior deposits in Canada. The first ship-load of ore left Borwick Rails harbour in 1859, the mineral being taken over the sands on a wooden causeway and, by the turn of the following decade, it looked as if the Hodbarrow enterprise would be profitable. The *Ulverston Advertiser* of 17th May 1860 commented that "the enterprising spirit of Mr Barratt in searching for iron ore at Hodbarrow, Millom seems a fair way of being crowned with success". During 1861 and 1862 the company built a timber jetty at Crab Marsh Point and a tramway, believed to be of 3ft gauge, was laid to connect it to the mine, the *Ulverston Mirror* of 7th June 1862 reporting the first cargo of ore being shipped from the new pier. These early cargoes were destined for South Wales and Brymbo in North Wales. *The North Lonsdale Magazine and Lake District Miscellany* noted in 1867 that

Since the recent fortunate discovery of a valuable bed of rich iron ore, at Hodbarrow, ... the natural harbour of Borwick Rails has been suddenly called into use, and a pier erected, so that almost every tide brings in or takes out numbers of vessels loaded with mineral, the busy little steam tugs adding to the general activity. Immense quantities of cockles of a very large size were gathered on the sands at one time, but they have been exterminated.

In 1862 the mining company sought quotes from the Whitehaven & Furness Junction Railway for the carriage of ore to the Whitehaven area and in September the following

Hodbarrow pier looking towards Black Combe before the First World War. Borwick Rails harbour can be seen on the left, on the right iron ore schooners are sitting in the Duddon channel adjacent to the pier and the funnel of a Hodbarrow tug can be discerned at the end of the pier. The complex trackwork with double and single slips is worthy of inspection. The tracks leading off to the left headed south-west across the Mains to the mine and those to the right led to the other end of the pier.

Photo: Peter Holmes Collection

Hodbarrow - A Great Mine (1855 - 1968)

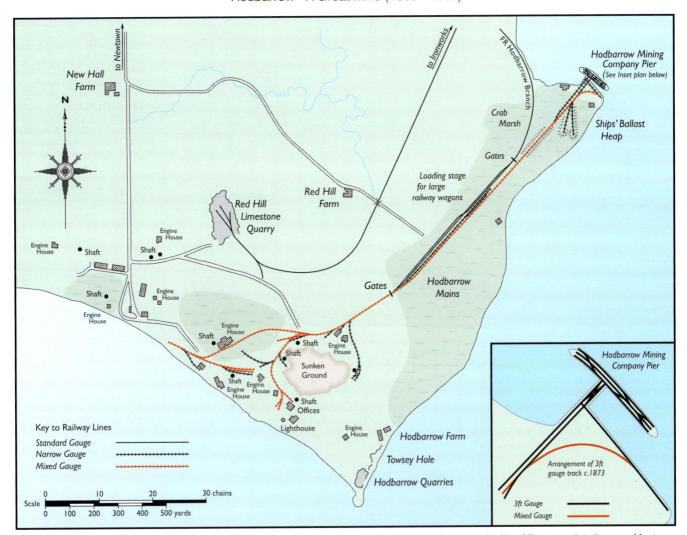

Hodbarrow Mines 1873 By this time new shafts were moving westwards towards Steel Green as the New Mine came into its own. Most of the original narrow gauge track had been converted to mixed gauge, although the pier was still exclusively narrow gauge. The coastline north-west of Hodbarrow Point had yet to be changed by the various barriers.

Drawn by Alan Johnstone, based on a map in the CRA Collection.

year sought reduced rates from Holborn Hill to Workington. The W&FJR directors agreed to 2s 10d (about 14p) per ton, provided it was carried in the mining company's wagons and in full train loads. Still the Hodbarrow partners were not satisfied and in November 1863, following an interview between Henry Cook, the W&FJR secretary, and John Barratt, the railway company approved orders for work to be done at Holborn Hill to accommodate loading "considerable quantities [of ore] to Workington". However, by February 1864 the W&FJR Board noted that the Hodbarrow company was not putting as much traffic on to the railway as promised and that consequently the then-current reduced rates offered would be withdrawn at the end of that month. Perhaps the threatened increase galvanised the mining company into sending more ore by rail for, in March, the W&FJR Board directed "an additional through shunt to be put in at Holborn Hill station to facilitate the loading of ore". However, the majority of the mine's output continued to be shipped from the pier at Crab Marsh Point. Table 3 shows some comparative annual tonnages for rail and sea between 1864 and 1872 and it can be seen that, despite the opening of the W&FJR's Hodbarrow branch in 1867 (see Chapter 6), the majority of the mine's output still went by sea. Shipping from its own pier was highly profitable to the company and served its traditional markets, reached by sea. It is recorded that, on a single day in 1892, eight ships loaded 4,400 tons from the pier and a further 610 tons went by rail.

Once the connecting line to Holborn Hill was completed in 1867, a loading stage was built on Hodbarrow Mains for transhipment between narrow gauge and standard gauge wagons. Thomas Hunter's quotation of 13th March that year for the construction of 591 yards of track and the ore wharf amounted to just over £543. By 1872 much of the Hodbarrow company's mileage between the mines and the pier had become mixed gauge, although the pier itself continued to be served solely by the narrow gauge. The narrow gauge system eventually fell out of use around 1877.

The large tonnage which left Hodbarrow by sea required the company to invest in its own tug to assist schooners through the treacherous Duddon channel and in November 1862 the first, *Voltigeur*, entered service. She was a wooden paddle steamer, built in Middlesbrough in 1851 and registered to William Barratt and Nathaniel Caine in Liverpool in 1862. However, she was not to last long due to her lack of manoeuvrability and the fact that she was reported to have leaked: she was scrapped in 1866, and her replacement, *Duddon*, another paddle steamer and built in iron by Harland & Wolff in Belfast, was launched in February of that year. The company felt that a second vessel was required to cover for the *Duddon* when she was out of service and so in 1870 bought another second-hand ship, the wooden tug *Prince Albert*. This vessel, built thirty years previously, had served the Whitehaven Harbour Trust for many years before arriving at Hodbarrow. She needed reboilering but when work started it was realised that there were further faults and it was decided to scrap her. A brand new tug, *Borwick Rails,* built in Liverpool, joined *Duddon* in 1871 and the pair worked turn about for the next 30 years until, in 1901, *Duddon* was overhauled and *Borwick Rails* was sold for scrap. Despite being deemed life-expired, *Borwick Rails* went on to work for the Whitehaven Harbour Trust and was eventually scrapped on

Table 3 Tonnages of iron ore moved from Hodbarrow by sea and rail 1864-1872

	1864	1865	1868	1869	1872
Tons by vessel	162,740	116,851	131,402	131,449	151,152
Tons by rail	24,675	513	56,014	67,256	57,510

Chapter Three

Rock House and the lighthouse erected in 1866 overlooked the original coastline near Hodbarrow Point. The light gave vessels much-needed guidance through the changing and difficult main channel of the Duddon which was buoyed. It fell into disuse after the construction of its replacement on the Outer Barrier. Rock House was used as offices and the remains of the windmill, to the left of the mast, are reputed to have been used as a gunpowder store in the mine's early days.

Photo: Stephe Cove Collection

Teesside in 1927. The last addition, *Hardback*, built in steel by Rennoldson in South Shields, was launched in 1901 and arrived at Hodbarrow in the same year. As noted below, the mine closed due to lack of orders in 1921 and consequently it was decided to sell both *Duddon* and *Hardback*. Little interest was expressed during this difficult period and it was not until 1923 that *Hardback* was sold, surviving until broken up at Seaham, County Durham in 1958. *Duddon* remained as the port tug until 1936 when she was finally scrapped after an incredible 70 years' service at Hodbarrow.

Up until 1871, other than its tugs, the company had no vessels of its own but in that year the directors suggested forming a shipping association. The company would own the largest share and by 1874 the Duddon Shipping Association, as it became, owned some 17 schooners, the first of which was the Ulverston–built *Burns and Bessie*. The mining company's secretary was always listed as the managing owner of the Association's vessels but ships' shares were widely distributed amongst members of the local community. Many ships were employed on a triangular service, taking ore from the Duddon to South Wales, coal from there to Ireland and finally pit props back to the Duddon. Additionally, prodigious quantities of coal necessary for pumping water out of the mine and for winding the ore were unloaded at the pier. The *Whitehaven News* of 15th March 1886 reports "as many as 30 to 40 vessels at a time lying near the pier for iron ore and iron ore only", although these would not all have been owned by the mining company. Borwick Rails harbour cleared 1,457 vessels during 1867 and the company maintained stockpiles at Ellesmere Port and Saltney, from where ore could be supplied to North Wales and the Midlands by canal and rail. The schooners were strongly built to cope with the dense haematite in the hold and the necessity to take the ground in a tidal harbour, resulting in many of them having extremely long lives. Even so, several vessels were lost at sea and the entry to the Duddon over the broad bar that crossed the mouth of the channel, and which rendered the entrance precarious when the tides were low, caused the loss of three of them. By 1922 all the schooners owned by the Duddon Shipping Association had

This card was posted in 1913 and depicts paddle tug Duddon *at her regular berth at the end of the Hodbarrow pier, which was constructed between 1861 and 1862.* Duddon *cost the mining company £3,800 in 1866. An event is taking place in the Crab Marsh inlet. Anderson's boat yard made yachts, cutters, fishing boats and dinghies to launch to the right of this view. Might this be one of their vessels in the foreground?*

Photo: Bill Myers Collection

Hodbarrow - A Great Mine (1855 - 1968)

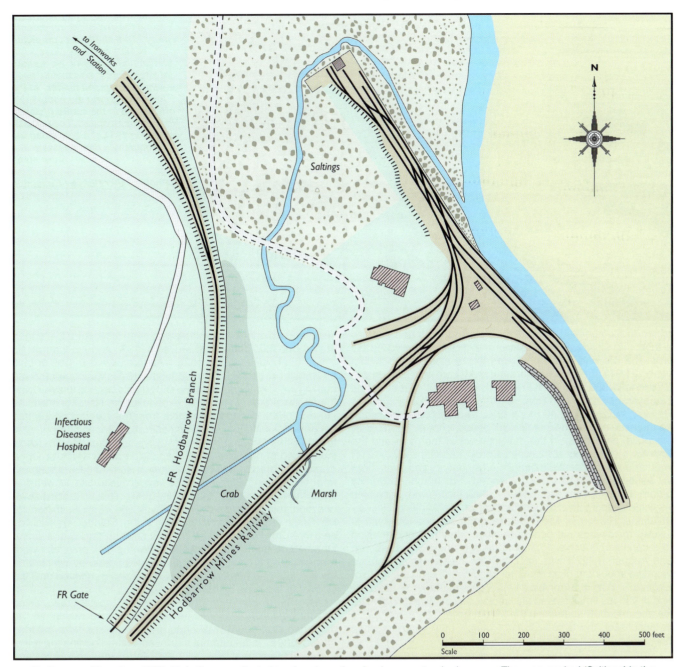

Hodbarrow Pier circa 1900 Note the complicated trackwork on the pier, by now standard gauge. The area marked 'Saltings' is the original natural harbour of Borwick Rails which pre-dated the Hodbarrow and ironworks piers. The FR gate marked the end of the railway company's Hodbarrow branch.
Drawn by Alan Johnstone, based on an Ordnance Survey Map.

been sold as the company struggled through the great slump which had closed the mine temporarily and which had resulted in the tugs being put up for sale.

Even while he was still employed as the mining company's first secretary, William Postlethwaite (1835-1910) was building a fleet of his own and by 1878 he had 22 vessels. By the time of his retirement from the mining company, Postlethwaite had amassed 26 ships, the second largest fleet of coasting schooners in the country. He also went into partnership with Amlwch ship owner and builder, William Thomas, who opened a subsidiary of his Anglesey yard at Borwick Rails in 1870. The first vessel built by the new concern was the Duddon Shipping Association's *Nellie Bywater*, launched in 1873; as testament to her sound construction, she survived until 1951. Apart from the link with the Hodbarrow Mining Company via Postlethwaite and the Duddon Shipping Association, William Thomas & Co built three wooden steamers for the Lady Kate Steamship Company. This was largely owned by Thomas Massicks from the adjacent ironworks (see Chapter 4) and in which Postlethwaite was also a partner. The Steamship Company was registered on 13th June 1881 but only enjoyed a brief existence before being wound up at Thomas' offices at Amlwch on 9th April 1886. After building three schooners, ownership of the shipyard passed to the Jones brothers, Hugh and Micaiah, in 1886. It was renamed the *Duddon Shipbuilding Company*, which continued to focus on repairs and the building of four more sailing vessels. The last one, fittingly a schooner for the Duddon Shipping Association named after one of John Barratt's relatives, was the *Emily Barratt*. She was launched in 1913, like her predecessors, sideways into the Duddon from the yard at the seaward end of the Hodbarrow pier. This vessel, the last schooner to be built in England, survived until as late as 1999, when she was reluctantly broken up by the Dock Museum in Barrow.

Returning to the activities below ground, even though the mine was proving to be extremely successful, prospecting continued and in 1868 the discovery of the main ore deposit further west, and which became known as the New Mine, was to dwarf the earlier efforts at the Old Mine. The fabulously rich mine that ultimately yielded around 25 million tons of high grade haematite was about to enter its heyday. In 1868 the *Ulverston Mirror* noted that thick deposits of ore had been discovered while drilling a well behind some cottages at Mainsgate (Mains is a north country word signifying land attached to a mansion or estate) and continued prophetically, "this will prove a very fortunate well for the parties concerned". Hodbarrow was producing more than a quarter of all the ore

Chapter Three

Hodbarrow No 1, or William, pit around the end of the nineteenth century. This shaft was completed in 1881 and was close to an earlier, unsuccessful, No 1 shaft. In later years it was mainly used for winding men and timber. In the left distance are the company's offices and in the centre distance Hodbarrow Hospital. The hospital closed in 1934 at a time when the company's finances were in a poor state.

Photo: Peter Holmes Collection

mined in Cumberland by 1872 and by 1883 this had risen to a third. To illustrate the extent of the mine's activities at this time, the ore output for 1878 warrants a closer look: in that year 121,914 tons (44%) were shipped from the pier on the Duddon, 61,589 tons (22%) made the short rail journey to the nearby ironworks, 87,069 tons (32%) were carried over Furness Railway metals and 4,400 tons (2%) were disposed of locally. As the mine approached its "heroic" period, another inordinately influential personality in the development of the mine and the new town arrived in 1872, when Cedric Vaughan (1841-1911) was appointed deputy manager. Vaughan, who was born in Ashby-de-la-Zouch, had attended Edinburgh University before being articled to Robert Stephenson and becoming Assistant Locomotive Superintendent of the Midland Railway at Derby. His former Midland colleagues seemed to be rather lukewarm towards his departure when, during a presentation to recognise his achievements at the Midland Hotel, Derby on 2nd August 1872, it was said that "he has accepted a more lucrative appointment as manager of some mines in the north of England". Within three years he became manager of the mine and at various times served as director, secretary and chairman. He became a JP and sat on the Millom Local Board, as well as its successor, the Urban District Council, until trade unionism and public opinion eventually forced him out.

For the first few years, the narrow gauge railway line from the Old Mine to Crab Marsh was worked by horses but an 0-4-0T locomotive appeared from the Lilleshall Company in 1866, the locomotive being delivered in two sections and completed at Hodbarrow. It lasted until the demise of the narrow gauge system around 1877. By this time the company's first standard gauge locomotive had been at work for five years, the second locomotive had arrived in 1874 and *Hodbarrow No 3* had been delivered in 1876. All three were 0-4-0STs built by Hunslet in Leeds. Throughout the 1870s the company was making sufficient profit from the Old Mine to be able to overcome the financial drain incurred in expanding the New Mine and by the end of the decade the output from the early workings had become insignificant. As mining operations moved further west toward Steel Green, so the railway system expanded to follow the sinking of new pits. Such expansion required the ordering of more locomotives, with *Hodbarrow Nos 4* and *5* appearing from Hunslet in 1880 and 1882 respectively, and *Hodbarrow No 6* from Neilson in Glasgow in 1890. This last locomotive, affectionately nicknamed *Snipey*, was one of six built (two for the South Eastern Railway, one for the Caledonian Railway and three for industrial use) by the Scottish firm with a crane mounted on top of the smokebox. No more locomotives were required by the company for another 40 years, by which time the first four had been scrapped. *Nos 5* and *6* survived until the closure of the mine in 1968.

By 1880 exploitation of the main ore deposit drew mining activity perilously close to the shore line and reluctantly an unrobbed strip of ore was left to prevent the sea from entering the workings. In an attempt to prevent water flooding the mine, a clay embankment was built between Hodbarrow Point and Haverigg during 1880. Four years later this was replaced by a substantial timber revetment but this, in turn, was found to be inadequate. In 1888 contracts were signed with Messrs Lucas & Aird, the same contractors who had built the wooden barrier, for a concrete sea wall to the designs of the eminent engineer

This view at Hodbarrow is believed to be Hunslet No 244, Hodbarrow No 4, supplied new in 1880. It is probably standing on the elevated coal road behind the engine house at No 5 pit. The photograph was taken in the early 1920s.

Photo: Joe Walker Collection via MJ Lee

This works photograph depicts **Hodbarrow No 6**, *as delivered from Neilson's in Glasgow in 1890. Nicknamed* Snipey, *the loco survived until the end of mining operations in 1968 when it was preserved. In later years the cab was enclosed, no doubt much to the liking of crews working in the windswept wastes of the haematite mines.* Photo: CRA Library Ref M01079

Sir John Coode (1816-1892). Two thirds of a mile in length and costing £106,311 (about £6.5 million in 2012), the Inner Barrier, as it later became known, comprised a combination of a 50ft high concrete wall facing the sea backed by an embankment of clay, sealed on the inner side by a wall and trench of puddled clay. Many men made redundant from the ironworks as a consequence of the bitter five month strike of 1889 found work as labourers on the sea wall construction project. The final block was laid on 23rd October 1890 and made available some five million tons of ore under 26 acres of the sea bed. Lucas & Aird constructed a network of temporary tramways, along which materials and machinery were transported from the pier or from Millom station using three of the Manning Wardle 0-4-0STs favoured by these contractors for their sea defence works and harbour construction projects. The new barrier was highly regarded as a work of civil engineering as well as a local attraction and in 1892 the *Millom Gazette* observed that the wall afforded a "splendid promenade during the summer season"; people were allowed on from 9-00am to sunset and a mining company employee was always in charge to give information to visitors.

The peak year for Cumbrian ore tonnage mined was 1882 and Lothian Bell, writing in 1884, stated "the only important deposits in Great Britain of native oxide of iron fit for steel-making as now commonly practised are those in Cumberland and Furness". During the 1880s the iron ore trade generally began to suffer from the import of Spanish ore which was of similar quality to the Cumbrian variety but was cheaper to extract; it was sufficiently close to the surface to be quarried and labour costs were less than in the UK. The Hodbarrow directors responded to the challenge by seeking new markets close to home and abroad, meaning that output continued to rise throughout the decade. In truth, the development of the basic process for making steel had reduced the need for the high iron (up to 60%), low phosphorus Cumbrian haematite and allowed the use of quarried ironstone from Cleveland, Northamptonshire and Lincolnshire, where the iron content was only around 30%.

There was still plenty of ore to be obtained from the mine, with annual output never below 400,000 tons up to the turn of the century. In 1896 it is recorded that there were 1,117 men employed underground with 318 above ground: this compared with a figure of between 500 and 600 men at the

In the centre No 5 (Arnold) pit sits on the edge of the Broken Ground and Annie Lowther pit is on the right hand skyline. The devastation to the landscape caused by 'top slicing' is clear to see and running across the Broken Ground in front of the pump houses are the remains of the original timber revetment.

Photograph held at Cumbria Archives and Local Studies Centre, Barrow.

Chapter Three

Messrs Lucas & Aird secured the £106,311 contract for the Inner Barrier in July 1888 and this photograph shows the wall nearing the end of its construction. One of the contractor's Manning Wardle 0-4-0 saddle tanks draws a train of the firm's wagons. The last block was laid on 23rd October 1890 and it is claimed that the wall was a great place for picnics and concerts.

Photo: Stephe Cove Collection

nearby ironworks. However, in 1898 seawater and sand broke into the mine near the Inner Barrier, causing the wall to crack. Since the company had already realised that the ore body extended under the sea beyond the barrier, a decision was made to construct yet another sea wall, encompassing an even larger area of coastline. The contract went to John Aird & Company, Lucas & Aird's successors, and work started at the Haverigg end in April 1900.

The Outer Barrier was over a mile and a quarter in length and stretched from Haverigg to Hodbarrow Point, although the mining company would have enclosed an even larger area had the Board of Trade not insisted that to do so would affect navigation of the Duddon. Costing some £560,000 (equivalent to more than £32 million at 2012 prices), it consisted of a limestone rubble bank, backed with clay in which was fixed steel or timber piling. On the landward side of the clay bank was a further bank of slag or more limestone rubble and the seaward side of the outer limestone bank was protected by blocks of limestone and concrete. The whole structure was designed to be flexible in order to adapt itself to subsidence, unlike the Inner Barrier which was rigid and broke up as the ground beneath it gave way. The barrier was a spectacular engineering project, consuming 621,000 tons of limestone and, when building was at its height, some 1,200 men were employed. It can be imagined that pressure on housing in the town was immense during the period of the wall's construction and, in July 1901, 15 Furness Railway employees petitioned the Railway's general manager to build cottages due to the scarcity of accommodation because of Aird's contract. Plans were submitted showing twelve homes at an estimated cost of £3,100 but the FR Traffic and Works Committee declined to build them. As they had done during construction of the Inner Barrier, Aird's once more laid an extensive network of temporary track and 13 of the company's Manning Wardle saddle tank locomotives were put to work. Table 4 is taken from *The Times* of 30th June 1906 and lists the surplus equipment to be sold by auction at the contractor's depot at Millom on completion of the Hodbarrow contract.

Table 4 Equipment to be sold by John Aird & Co 1906
Four six and four wheel locomotives
Three steam navvies
Three 25 ton block setting Goliaths
Two 12 ton steam cranes
Rails, points, crossings, fishplates, sleepers
270 end tip wagons
35 high and low side end and side tip wagons
14 ballast trucks
One break [sic] van
16 25 ton concrete block trolleys
26 platelayers and other trolleys
19 pipe trolleys

Aird had contracts worldwide and some of the locomotives involved in building the Outer Barrier eventually ended up in Singapore.

The disastrous consequences of ruthless top-slicing are demonstrated by the remains of the ruined Inner Barrier. The enormous hollow largely on the landward side of the wall was caused by the collapse of the surface into the workings of the main productive ore deposit at Hodbarrow.

Photo: Stephe Cove Collection

Hodbarrow - A Great Mine (1855 - 1968)

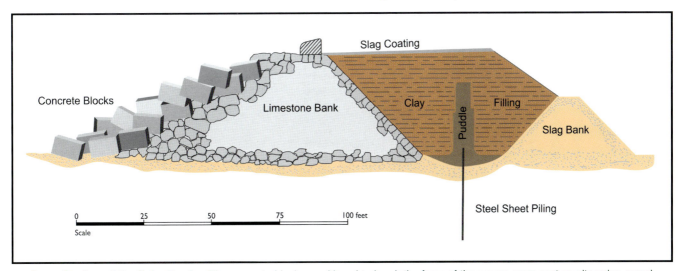

Cross Section of the Outer Barrier The concrete blocks, positioned to break the force of the waves, were cast on site using gravel from the beach; clay was dug from the surface of the mine; limestone came from quarries only a few hundred yards inland and slag was obtained from the ironworks.
Drawn by Alan Johnstone and author from a drawing held at Cumbria Archives and Local Studies Centre, Barrow.

On 27th April 1900, two of John Aird's Manning Wardle saddle tanks and a brake van not unlike products of the Furness Railway, form the background as Harry Arnold, the Hodbarrow chairman, cuts the first sod of the Outer Barrier project at the Haverigg end of the site.

Photo: Millom Discovery Centre Collection

Work on the Outer Barrier at Hodbarrow nears completion in April 1905. One of the Goliath block-setting cranes is seen in the background. Harry Arnold laid the last block on 13th April 1905. When construction was at its height around 1,200 men were employed by John Aird & Company.

Photograph held at Cumbria Archives and Local Studies Centre, Barrow.

35

Chapter Three

The Outer Barrier nearing completion in April 1905. In the foreground are seen some of the many 25 ton concrete blocks positioned in tiers on the seaward side. Two of Aird's three-plank wagons with dumb buffers are in the centre of the picture and one of the contractor's Manning Wardle K Class 0-6-0STs is attached to a break [sic] van.

Photograph held at Cumbria Archives and Local Studies Centre, Barrow.

The sea was excluded on 20th July 1904 and the barrier was finished on 1st October. Once the work on the contract was completed on 13th April 1905, some 170 additional acres of land were newly reclaimed from the sea and the Inner Barrier was allowed to collapse into the mine workings below. The completion of the new barrier allowed an extension of mining into the area formerly beneath the sea and between 1905 and 1909 output never fell below half a million tons a year, a record that was never to be beaten. Hodbarrow was now raising as much ore as all the remaining mines in Cumberland combined; its continuing success was in contrast to the other mines in Cumberland and Furness where output was beginning to fall sharply as the iron ore bodies were worked out. The combined output of the Furness mines had peaked at 1.4 million tons a year in 1882, but had fallen below 400,000 tons by 1908. In the period up to the First World War output from Hodbarrow began to fall, although increased demand during the hostilities, when the Ministry of Munitions ran the mine, caused it to rise again: proposals were made in March 1917 for an increase in output of 3,300 tons a week by supplementing the workforce with 400 prisoners of war who were to live in a specially-built camp. There is no record of the camp having being built but it is known that Scottish miners were employed to maintain production. In 1919 the Ministry of Munitions gave up its requisition of Hodbarrow but, with the war over, the period of prosperity abruptly ended, never to return.

The years following the war were difficult for the iron industry in Furness and West Cumberland; on 29th January 1921 the mine closed completely due to there being no orders and did not reopen until June that year. During the next five years it was not possible to work the mine for a full year and, despite some revival in fortune after the 1926 General Strike, output fell below 10,000 tons in 1933. Even though the glory days were over, there still remained one final chapter in the Hodbarrow story – the sinking of the last shaft at Moorbank was started in August 1928 and completed in early 1931. Moorbank, or No 11, was to see the mine through to its final closure in 1968. However, its location, almost at Haverigg and requiring a half mile extension to the railway from William Pit round the seaward side of the Hodbarrow offices at Steel Green, made the costs of moving its output to the exchange sidings on the Mains greater than from the older shafts.

By the 1930s the oldest locomotives, *Hodbarrow Nos 1* to *4*, had gone and a replacement *No 3* arrived in the form of a Peckett 0-4-0ST of Class M5 (works No 1719) in 1930, followed by a much more powerful 0-4-0ST, *No 4*, (works No 1647 of Class E) from the same manufacturers in 1933. The company's first second-hand purchase arrived in 1934 in the shape of an Avonside 0-4-0ST, works No 1563 of 1908, from a dealer in South Wales and which took the identity of *Hodbarrow No 2*. In August of that year the loco shed adjacent to the main workshops blew down in a gale and for the next 34 years locomotives were stabled in the open, close to the site of the original shed.

The last working shaft at Hodbarrow was Moorbank or No 11, seen here on 30th March 1968, immediately after closure. Sinking of this shaft began in 1928 and was not completed until 1931. The houses in the background, some of which were destroyed by enemy action in 1941, were part of the mining company's Steel Green estate.

Photo: Peter Holmes

36

Hodbarrow - A Great Mine (1855 - 1968)

The underground lines at Hodbarrow are beyond the scope of this book but, for completeness, it is appropriate to include this view of 1ft 10in gauge Ruston & Hornsby 170194 of 1934, probably photographed at Moorbank pit bottom on the 60 fathom level shortly after delivery from Lincoln.

Photo: Millom Discovery Centre Collection

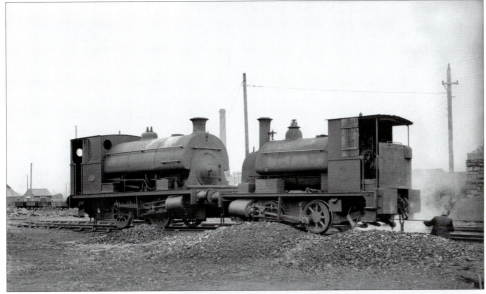

On 29th July 1947 Peckett E Class No 1647 of 1933 and Avonside No 563 of 1908 share the primitive loco facilities at Hodbarrow. The two Bristol-built locos arrived in Millom within twelve months of each other, the Peckett coming new and the Avonside from South Wales. Weighing nearly 35 tons loaded, the Peckett was found too heavy for Hodbarrow's indifferent trackwork and was out of use by 1959. It went to the ironworks in exchange for Kerr Stuart 4009 in the mid 1960s.

Photo: Kidderminster Railway Museum

The Avonside crosses the road leading to the Hodbarrow workshops with loaded hoppers from Moorbank to Millom Ironworks. Lowscales and Black Combe dominate the distance and the grassed-over Red Hills slag bank is on the right.

Photo: Dave Cousins

37

Chapter Three

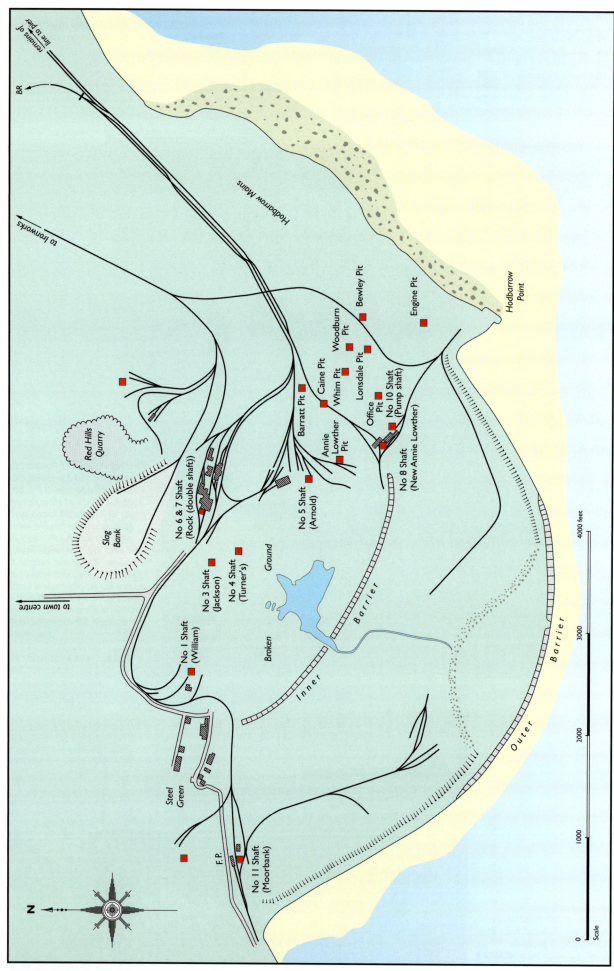

Hodbarrow Mine circa 1950 This shows the maximum extent of the operation but by this time the only shafts lifting ore were Nos 6, 8 and 11, although other shafts were used to pump sand in and water out of the mine. The ironworks line to Red Hills is separate from the Hodbarrow system, although they join near the workshops and near Hodbarrow Point where the route was used to tip slag behind the Outer Barrier.
Drawn by Alan Johnstone, based on an Ordnance Survey Map.

Hodbarrow - A Great Mine (1855 - 1968)

On a wet day at Hodbarrow in the 1950s Hunslet No 299 of 1882 is prominent. On the right stands one of the Pecketts: the rear of the cab looks to be homemade but was, no doubt, appreciated by the crew on days like this when the wide expanses near the sea could be very inhospitable.

Photo: CRA Library Ref SHI209

From the mid-1930s, as the Depression ended and the country's re-armament programme got underway, production at Hodbarrow started to increase again and haematite raised from the far-flung remains of the once-great mine was again in demand. The Ministry of Supply took over the mine in 1940 and in that same year the last shipments from the pier at Crab Marsh were noted, the number of vessels using the pier having dropped to only two or three a week during the 1930s. After 1945 production continued to decline, although nowhere near as sharply as it had done after the First World War, but the unwelcome spectre of nationalisation under Clement Attlee's Labour government was looming. From 15th February 1951, the Iron and Steel Act (1949) was implemented and the Hodbarrow Mining Company became part of the Iron & Steel Corporation of Great Britain. It is interesting to note that on the eve of nationalisation, nearly a hundred years after Barratt and Caine formed the company, 14.2% of the Hodbarrow shares were still owned by people from Devon and Cornwall. By the end of 1958 the now-Conservative government had returned 70% of the iron and steel companies to private hands, Hodbarrow being sold to the Millom Hematite Ore & Iron Company Ltd in that year. However the mine in 1958 was only a shadow of its former self and, after the Red Hill deposit ceased to be worked in October (via No 6 and No 8 shafts),

only Moorbank remained in production. Included in the sale was Millom Ironworks and so, for the first time in nearly a century, the two Millom iron companies were one. Hodbarrow had been the only iron ore mine in Cumberland and Furness that had not been bought by one of the smelting companies. The amalgamation made sense in that the Millom works was the mine's best customer and, from 1964, only customer. By the time of its closure on 22nd March 1968, when raising ore had finally become uneconomic, only 103 men were left working at the mine and the final year's tonnage raised was little more than 20,000. In the end, the difficult shape of the remaining deposits, the expense of necessary sand filling, the increased cost of materials, pumping and wages allied to shorter working hours and extra holidays brought over 100 years of mining at Hodbarrow to a close.

For most of the mine's history the ore had been raised by "top slicing", a process in which ore was won from the top of the deposit downwards. As the extraction went deeper the ground above was allowed to collapse into the workings, leaving characteristic extensive areas of "broken ground". However, the sudden abnormal demand for ore during the First World War led to the worked-out parts of the mine being in-filled with sand to avoid the risk of water entering the workings as the ground above collapsed more quickly than

Snipey's crew smile for the camera in March 1968, shortly before Hodbarrow's final demise. The large rear overhang with the firebox behind the axle was to counterbalance the weight of the crane on the smokebox.

Photo: Frank Atkinson

Chapter Three

The extensive workshops at Hodbarrow are seen just after closure. Three of the ancient side-tipping wagons await their fate on the left. The preservation of all this as a working museum would have been a tremendous attraction in the area but it was probably an impossible dream. As well as the Avonside, the Hunslet and the crane tank, together with wagons and steam grabs, the buildings would have housed industrial and railway relics from the Whitehaven and Furness areas. The preservation group needed to raise £800 to ensure a comprehensive selection of equipment but, in the event, this proved impossible.

Photo: Peter Holmes

under normal rates of extraction. After 1922 the company began to extract ore from the bottom upwards and perfected a way of introducing a sand/water mixture into the worked-out cavities below so that more ore could be extracted with no danger of the ground above collapsing into the workings. Sand was gathered from Marsh Quarry behind the Outer Barrier from what had once been the beach and conveyed in sets of three 4½ cubic yard capacity side-tipping wagons of ancient design to a service shaft north of Moorbank: in latter days, at least, this duty was entrusted to the Avonside 0-4-0ST, *Hodbarrow No 2*. Spreading over an area of about a square mile, Hodbarrow presented a unique, almost lunar, landscape of hollows, abandoned workings and grass-covered railway lines. The railway system had grown in piecemeal fashion to serve the various new workings, eventually totalling some 40 miles of track, and the journey from Moorbank to the exchange sidings on the Mains was around two miles. During post-war years the daily Moorbank ore trains comprised around seven wagons, hauled by the Avonside to the sidings where locomotives from Hodbarrow, the ironworks and the main line shared each other's tracks between the railway company gate at the eastern end and the Hodbarrow gate to the west. One ex-Hodbarrow employee recalled that these gates were demolished on more than one occasion. Main line locomotives as big as Stanier Class 5MT 4-6-0s came as far as the Hodbarrow gate and Hodbarrow locomotives went as far as the FR/LMS/BR gate. Ironworks locomotives normally travelled no further west than the Hodbarrow gate but sometimes went on to the Hodbarrow system to turn on the triangle outside the fitting shop.

Shortly before the mine closed an ambitious scheme was floated to preserve as much as possible of the historic railway equipment. The preservationists intended to establish a working museum in the extensive buildings then still standing and to purchase the remaining locomotives, together with some of the unique wagons and steam grab cranes. Sadly, the scheme proved to be over-optimistic and the Hodbarrow Preservation Group had to settle for the Avonside (for £160) and a couple of wagons. After a nomadic existence, this locomotive is still in existence at the Foxfield Railway in Staffordshire and carries the appropriate, if non-authentic, name *Millom*. Following time at Steamtown, Carnforth, the wagons made their way to Beamish Museum in 2008 and one of them, thought to date from around 1880, is under restoration in 2012. *Snipey* went to the Lytham Motive Power Museum, which is now closed but the locomotive is believed to be still there. The Hunslet returned to its manufacturers in Leeds, being put on a plinth outside the works, then went to the National Railway Museum but was last seen dismantled at the Armley Mills Museum in Leeds. The stored Kerr, Stuart was scrapped following closure of the mine. The most modern locomotive by far was the 1946-built Hudswell Clarke, the penultimate locomotive to arrive at Hodbarrow. This 0-4-0ST had been at the Eskmeals Gun Range (see Chapter 6) from 1948 until it was sold to Millom Ironworks in February 1957, where it was stored before being transferred to Hodbarrow in 1963. When the mine closed it returned briefly to the ironworks and when that, in turn, closed was bought for preservation, the plan being for a steam centre in Millom goods yard. Although the locomotive was steamed in the goods yard and ran down the Hodbarrow branch as far as the closed ironworks during 1969, the steam centre project foundered and on 21st March 1970, 1742 was loaded on to a low-loader for transport to the Quainton Road preservation scheme in Buckinghamshire (now the Buckinghamshire Railway Centre). There it was eventually returned to working order, like the Avonside bearing the appropriate, but inauthentic, name *Millom*.

The story now goes back in time to 1865 in order to consider the other major player in the industrial development of south-west Cumberland. This will show that relationships between the Hodbarrow Mining Company and the owners of the Millom Ironworks were often far from convivial and so it seems appropriate that each is given the distinction of a chapter to itself.

Table 5 Hodbarrow Locomotives at closure in 1968			
Hodbarrow No	Builders	Works No	Built
5	Hunslet Engine Company	299	1882
6	Neilson & Company	4004	1890
2	Avonside Engine Company	1563	1908
1	Hudswell, Clarke & Company	1742	1946
11 *	Kerr, Stuart & Company	4009	1919

Stored out of use. Ex-Barrow Hematite Steel Co, ex-Millom Ironworks

Millom Ironworks (1867-1968)

Millom - second choice; the Whicham Mining Company; Millom and Askam; Spanish operations; mines in West Cumberland; North Lonsdale Ironworks; Millspray; motive power.

4

"the tall chimneys of Millom, wealthy through the riches of its ore beneath the sands"
　　　　　　　　　　　　WG Collingwood, 'The Lake Counties'

THE BUILDING of a modern coke-fuelled ironworks at Millom came rather late in the day compared with other such enterprises in Furness and West Cumberland: works had opened at Cleator Moor in 1841, at Workington (Oldside) in 1856, Harrington in 1857, Barrow in 1859 and Workington (West Cumberland) in 1862. Using finance largely provided by George Henry Horsfall (1824-1900) and other Liverpool businessmen, the Cumberland Iron Mining & Smelting Company (CIM&SC) was formed in 1862 and explored some fifteen sites between Maryport and Barrow for its ironworks. It eventually settled on a site at Mirehouse, near Whitehaven, with the intention of using iron ore from the West Cumberland mines. However, at a crucial stage in the negotiations with the land owner, the Second Earl of Lonsdale, consent was withheld and during July 1865 the company's managing director, Thomas Massicks (1832-1908), made arrangements to erect furnaces on a new 55 acre site on the edge of the Duddon estuary close to the developing Hodbarrow mine. Massicks was to become a pivotal figure in the development of the ironworks and the new town that was to spring up adjacent to it. Born at Bardsea, the son of an old family of landowners, he was educated in Kendal before obtaining an official position in the Whitehaven Harbour Trust. From 1860 onwards he was involved in haematite mining and colliery work in the Whitehaven district, which interests were eventually taken over by the CIM&SC. In 1866 he moved to Silecroft and in the following year to Millom, to live at *Duddon Villa*, newly-built close to the ironworks. From 1874 he lived in some style at *The Oaks*, between The Green and Hallthwaites and, such was his influence and power that, in 1875 he became the Millom Local Board's first chairman and a county magistrate in 1880. By 1884 he had styled himself Barlow-Massicks, apparently due to his mother insisting that Massicks' son, Thomas Jr, would not inherit her property without this appellation. He resigned as managing director of the ironworks in 1894, but continued as a director for a year or two and finally left *The Oaks* in 1900. Massicks really deserves better recognition in the town that he founded virtually single-handed.

Despite the unpromising nature of the marshy ground and lack of accommodation for the workforce, the site was well chosen. Apart from the prodigious quantities of iron ore at Hodbarrow, limestone was available from the nearby Redhills quarry leased to the company by Lord Lonsdale. There was plenty of room to dump slag; there was the possibility of shipping iron out and ore in and, above all, there were existing railway connections. The Whitehaven & Furness Junction Railway had opened throughout in 1850 (Chapter 2) and a branch line from Holborn Hill station to serve the nearby Hodbarrow mine had been authorised in the W&FJR's Act of June 1865; the new ironworks would be situated immediately adjacent to, and to the south-west of, this branch line. The West Cumberland coal was high in phosphorus and sulphur and thus coke produced from it was unsuited for use in blast furnaces with the local haematite (which had very low proportions of these two elements). The July 1861 opening of the South Durham & Lancashire Union Railway enabled the more suitable Durham coke to reach the area, albeit by a roundabout route via Stainmore Summit, Tebay and Carnforth. The building of the W&FJR was an absolutely necessary precursor to the development of the iron-making industry on the banks of the Duddon estuary and, as a consequence, to the building of the new town of Millom, as described in Chapter 5. In the early blast furnaces, production of one ton of pig iron needed around four tons of ore and coke and the movement of this material to the site was a critical issue in deciding upon a location. However, the cost of moving coke over such large distances was partially offset by the fact that Cumbrian furnaces used only 75% of the average fuel input of British furnaces at the time due to the extreme richness of the ore. As early as August 1865, Massicks was negotiating (in the event unsuccessfully) with the Hodbarrow company for all its output, this tension characterising the relationship between the two companies for most of the remainder of their existence. Construction of the works was rapid, a tramway was constructed to Redhills quarry and the first iron was produced from its two furnaces in September 1867, only two years after construction had begun. In the light of subsequent developments, it is interesting to note that the new plant was to have been called the *Duddon Ironworks* but instead *Millom* was chosen, even though no town of that name was then in existence. Two further furnaces followed almost immediately, rising to five by the end of 1869. By the early 1870s there were six, with five of them usually in blast, giving a maximum total daily output of nearly 100 tons. These early furnaces were open to the atmosphere at the top but progress in design led to them being replaced by four of higher capacity equipped with regenerative hot blast stoves as early as 1874, followed quickly by two more. Despite opposition from the mining company, a pier was constructed in 1872 immediately north-west of Hodbarrow pier but access to the pier by both rail and sea was awkward. To get from the furnaces to the pier, ironworks rail traffic had to cross the main

This photograph of Thomas Barlow-Massicks was included in a special supplement to the Millom Gazette of 24th April 1908 to accompany Massicks' obituary. Massicks made a fortune during the boom years at Millom but used his power and influence to the enormous advantage of the people in the developing new town.
　　　　　　　　Photo: Millom Discovery Centre Collection

41

Chapter Four

This view of the furnaces at Millom dates from around 1870 and shows an additional furnace under construction. Note the stacks of iron pigs in the foreground, the method of haulage and the early furnaces open to the atmosphere.

Photo: Bill Myers Collection

line company's Hodbarrow branch on the level, requiring some form of signalling. For many years this took the form of a simple cross bar signal which turned through 90° to indicate right of way, but in BR days it was replaced by a short range electrical indicator, rather like a small colour-light signal. The vagaries of the Duddon estuary made the approach to the pier by ship even more difficult but, once over the bar, captains could expect between 12 and 13 feet of water at spring tides and the only costs were 4d (about 1½p) payable to the Lord of the Manor. Constant dredging of the Duddon channel was necessary to permit vessels to access the pier and the sand thus raised was used in the pig beds, the moulds resembling suckling pigs into which the molten iron was run. The arrival of vessels from abroad meant that a hospital had to be built for isolating diseases brought in from foreign ports. This was constructed out of tarred timber and was situated in a remote spot on Hodbarrow Mains.

It fell out of use between the wars, eventually being burned down as a training exercise for the local fire brigade during the Second World War. Closer to the ironworks, near the end of the Hodbarrow branch, was another hospital, the red-painted infectious diseases (or isolation) hospital for inhabitants of the town who had contracted diseases such as scarlet fever and diphtheria, from which many never recovered.

The new company's first locomotive, an 0-4-0 well tank, was delivered from Fletcher, Jennings & Company at Lowca in May of the same year that the ironworks opened and a similar machine was delivered from the same source in 1869. As the works expanded through the 1870s and 1880s, more 0-4-0 and 0-6-0 tank locomotives were delivered from a variety of manufacturers, including Fox Walker, Peckett, Neilson and Barclay and, most unusually, a second-hand 2-4-0T came from the London & North Western Railway.

Neilson No 4690 was delivered new to Millom Ironworks in 1894 and survived there until scrapped in 1956. Given the local identity of Millom No 6, this loco spent some time on loan to Vickers-Armstrongs at Eskmeals Gun Range around 1938. The photograph was on a Neilson carte de visite.

Photo: Peter Holmes Collection

Millom Ironworks (1867 - 1968)

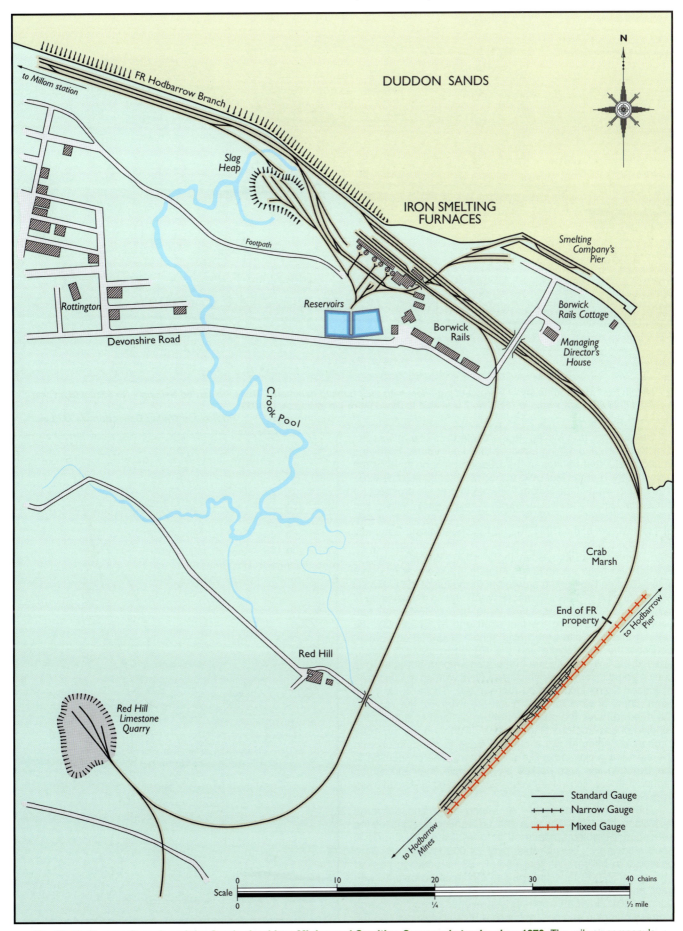

The FR Hodbarrow Branch and the Cumberland Iron Mining and Smelting Company's tracks circa 1870 The railway company's line passed immediately to the north-east of the works and various working agreements covered the adjacent sidings. Notice the smelting company's track to its pier crossing the FR lines on the level – a feature retained until closure.

Drawn by Alan Johnstone, based on a map in the CRA Collection.

Millom No 7 in the company of a group of pig-lifters with their hooked hammers. This loco carried Neilson's No 5210 and arrived from their Glasgow works in 1897. No 7 was sold to David Caird Ltd at Barrow in 1939.
Photo: Joe Walker Collection via MJ Lee.

Despite the "Iron Mining" in the company's title, it was not directly involved in mining activities until later years. Following unsuccessful test borings in the Duddon estuary, in 1879 the redoubtable Thomas Massicks turned his attentions some three miles north-west of the Millom furnaces in order to prospect for iron ore at Limestone Hall, just north of the Furness Railway line between Kirksanton and Silecroft. Initially run by a partnership of five directors of the CIM&SC, the Whicham Mining Company was formed in May 1880 (becoming a limited company from 29th December 1880). Speaking in 1890, Massicks claimed that he had been interested in searching for ore at this spot since 1863 or 1864 (even before the formation of the CIM&SC and confirming that his aspirations went beyond the smelting of iron). Once more, progress was rapid: by July 1879 work had commenced on sinking the first shaft and by September the second and third pits were being sunk. Following agreement between the landowners and the FR, the railway company opened the link from its line in the same month but nothing is known about locomotives which may have worked at Whicham, or indeed if any loco worked there at all. There would have been plenty of work for one, given the extent of the site and the need to move the quantities of ore out and coal in for the winding shafts and pumping engines. Furthermore, the 1895 Ordnance Survey shows a building close to the junction with the main line which looks like a loco shed. The connection to the Up Main line was worked by the single lever Kirksanton ground frame, which in later years was released by Annett's key from Silecroft signal box.

The first ore was raised in March 1880 and delivered to Millom, but later that year the first ominous signs of the subsequent problems appeared as one of the pits started to flood alarmingly. Despite this, over 24,000 tons of ore were delivered to Millom that year and in 1881 production peaked at around 50,000 tons but, due to increasing problems with sand and water entering the workings, no ore was raised at all during 1884. In 1889 work stopped altogether until two large Cornish pumping engines, one with a 90 inch cylinder and the other even larger at 100 inches, were shipped from Hayle in Cornwall to Barrow, taken by rail to Kirksanton and installed at No 8 pit the following year. There was then sufficient pumping equipment installed to lift a total of 5,700 gallons of water per minute. Optimism remained high: at the time the Whicham deposit was believed to be the largest virgin iron ore field in Cumberland and, with iron content at around 62%, it seemed

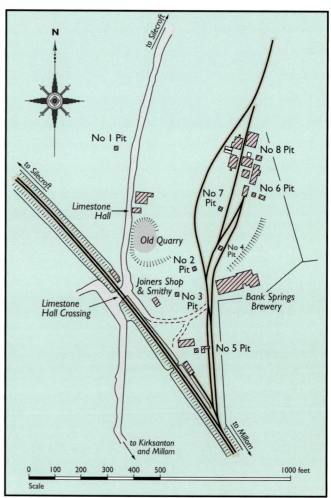

Whicham Mines shortly after closure in 1895 The extensive track layout could have required the use of a locomotive and the building close to the main line connection could well be an engine shed, but no records have been found of locomotives being used. In later years the track was cut back to serve the brewery.
Drawn by Alan Johnstone, based on an Ordnance Survey Map and personal correspondence from Lorraine Wilson.

Millom Ironworks (1867 - 1968)

This bottle label is a reminder of an industry long-associated with Kirksanton but which disappeared almost 60 years ago.   **Lorraine Wilson Collection**

set to rival Hodbarrow. From 1892 the CIM&SC had a financial interest in the Whicham mines but the high cost of pumping and the FR's rail transfer costs to Millom meant that Whicham ore was considerably more expensive than that bought from Hodbarrow. Eventually it was realised that the whole project had been an expensive failure: boring had passed through the main body of ore and loans taken out to fund the building of the huge pumps were called in. On 3rd September 1895 the mines were formally abandoned, and on 27th September the company went into voluntary liquidation, less than 5,000 tons having been raised in its final year. Not long afterwards Massicks severed his links with the ironworks, having lost much of his personal fortune in the Whicham venture. Two years later he attempted to revive the old Lonsdale Ironworks in Whitehaven as chairman and managing director of the new Lonsdale Hematite Smelting Company but this too failed. The Whicham mines stood disused until 1898, when the CIM&SC bought the plant and dismantled it, despite strong local rumours that the mines were about to be reopened by the Hodbarrow Mining Company.

At the south end of the Kirksanton site, adjacent to No 2 pit, was Bank Springs Brewery, founded by William Brockbank (1830-?) and his brother James Wilson Brockbank (1833-1904). William Brockbank appears as an innkeeper at Chapel Sucken in the 1858 *Post Office Directory* and in July 1863 the W&FJR directors had declined an offer from Messrs Brockbank of Kirksanton to purchase land at Holborn Hill station to build an inn. However it has not proved possible to determine the opening date of the brewery. Prior to 1878 James Brockbank had been involved with Bateman Wilson and William Brocklebank Walker in unsuccessful searches for iron ore in the immediate neighbourhood and he later became a director of the Whitehaven Hematite Iron & Steel Company Ltd. William Brockbank had been connected with the mining and shipping trade and had even arranged to secure the Kirksanton royalty from the Earl of Lonsdale but, fortunately as it turned out, failed to do so due to Lonsdale's agent missing his train to Furness Abbey. The Brockbanks took advantage of the rapid growth in population of Millom and district during the latter half of the nineteenth century, and were able to obtain licences for an increasing number of outlets. The brewery used the Whicham Mining Company siding connection to the main line, later cut back to access the brewery alone, and took its water from springs on Lacra Fell, the soft water hereabouts being particularly suitable for brewing. *Brockey's* was sold in between 20 and 30 pubs, hotels and off-licences in the Millom area. William Brockbank severed his connection with the brewery on becoming a JP in 1895 and ownership eventually passed to his brother's children. The connection to the brewery sidings was finally removed on 23rd March 1952 and the last brew was in July 1954, the brewery and pubs being bought by Matthew Brown of Blackburn. One of the few visible remains of mining activity at Kirksanton is the row of houses built for mine workers, Whicham Terrace, while the former brewery buildings, now Listed Grade II, have been converted into a private house and holiday accommodation.

Meanwhile, back in Millom, the Cumberland Iron Mining & Smelting Company (a limited company since 1872) was casting its eyes towards the Lancashire bank of the Duddon and buying into some of the Furness mining leases in yet another attempt to secure a controlled supply of haematite. Askam Ironworks, opened by the Furness Iron & Steel Company in the same year as the Millom works, was in financial difficulties and in 1879 the company went into liquidation. The following year a new concern, the Askam & Mouzell Iron Company, was formed and in 1882 the Millom company bought it out and became sole owner. The two concerns amalgamated on 23rd September 1890 to form the Millom & Askam Hematite Iron Company Limited (M&AHIC). The company's name was always spelled *Hematite* but elsewhere in this volume the name for the mineral form of iron (III) oxide is spelled *haematite*. Thomas Massicks, who had founded the Askam & Mouzell Iron Company and had been managing director of both companies since 1881, agreed to continue in the same role for five years in the new concern, having made considerable profit from the sales of his Askam shares. Most of this personal fortune was invested in a financially ruinous venture with David Caird to buy and re-open the Vulcan Works in Barrow to manufacture railway tyres. From around this time Massicks was also chairman and managing director of the Buttermere Green Slate Company as well as being principal owner of the Lady Kate Steamship Company: little wonder that his involvement in such a large number of enterprises caused many to wonder if he could carry out all his duties properly. Just as 1890 saw the end of the CIM&SC, so it saw the end of GH Horsfall's connection with the Millom works; Horsfall had been chairman of the company since its inception 25 years earlier and he took the opportunity of the amalgamation to retire. At the time of the amalgamation the assets of the new concern included the two ironworks, all the mine leases of the former Furness Iron & Steel Company, limestone quarries at Redhills and Goldmire (near Dalton) and 40% of the shares in the Whicham Mining Company. The works, mines and quarries were reported as possessing 18 locomotives and 249 mineral wagons in 1890. The influence of the Millom & Askam Company in the area may be judged by the fact that a strike over the employment of non-union men in the year before the full amalgamation led to between 6,000 and 7,000 men being out of work.

By the end of the nineteenth century the Millom & Askam Company was thriving: for the month of April 1898 the *Millom Gazette* reported 26 boats loading 10,900 tons of pig iron at the company's pier, whereas the combined total loaded at Whitehaven, Workington, Maryport, Barrow and Ulverston only amounted to 8,683 tons in the same period. When the pier extension was completed in February the following year, it was reported that around 20 vessels had berthed there in the first three days of opening. The new century found the M&AHIC in possession of 20 miles of private railways and in expansionist mood; profits were high and the works on the Cumberland bank of the Duddon estuary had been continuously modernised since its inception over 30 years previously. The company was able to pay an enormous 28% dividend on its ordinary shares in September 1900. However, changes were afoot that were to seriously undermine the viability of iron mining and smelting in Cumberland and Furness. After Cleveland, the area was the second most important iron-making district in the country, but it suffered from the disadvantage that coke for the furnaces had to be brought large distances, although this was not too great

Chapter Four

This pre-First World War photograph of Millom Ironworks is taken from the slag bank which dominated the eastern end of Newtown. The masts of a ship moored at the pier can just be seen to the right of the central chimney. One of the reasons for choosing this site for the ironworks was the ability to tip slag on the banks of the Duddon. Photo: Bill Myers Collection

a problem as long as Cumberland haematite continued to be essential for steel making. Due to its low phosphorus content, the local ore and iron produced from it were particularly suited to making steel by the process invented by Henry Bessemer (1813-1898) in 1856. However, from 1879, the development of Sidney Gilchrist Thomas' (1850-1885) *basic* process, in which a lining of limestone enabled high-phosphorus ores to be used in a converter or in the open hearth process, reduced the demand for the Cumbrian products. Production of Bessemer steel peaked in Britain in 1889 and, from then onwards, the iron industry in Furness and West Cumberland was in gradual, but ultimately terminal, decline. Barlow-Massicks was well aware of the threat and, speaking to striking men in 1889, he said, "The Middlesbrough people have succeeded in making basic steel out of the worst ore in the world and it has pretty well ruined the works of this country(side)". The brief

Ullbank No1 on the ironworks pier crossing on 25th March 1950. The loco was delivered new as Avonside No 1728 to Ullbank Mine in 1916, transferring to Florence No 1 after Ullbank's closure in 1919. The loco moved south to Millom Ironworks in 1948 subsequent to the Florence closure and was finally scrapped in 1961.
Photo: KJ Cooper 1378, Industrial Railway Society copyright

Millom Ironworks (1867 - 1968)

Taken from the bridge to Duddon Villa and the pier, this 30th March 1968 view of the Ironworks looking back towards the junction with the main line clearly shows how the Hodbarrow branch (on the right of the loaded wagons in the centre) passed straight through the middle of the site. The original works, built 100 years earlier, was confined to the left of the branch as seen here.
Photo: Peter Holmes

period during which Millom and the other ironworks in West Cumberland and Furness had been at the centre of European and world production of Bessemer steel was over by the last decade of the nineteenth century and the area would ultimately become painfully vulnerable to economic fluctuations due to its dependence on one industry. Only two World Wars, and consolidation as other works closed, were to keep the Millom concern going for as long as it did.

From around 1873/4 Spanish ore had been imported through Barrow docks and the Cumberland ports, but on 23rd February 1900, ever-anxious to ensure its own supply of iron ore, the M&AHIC went into partnership with the Coltness Iron Company Ltd of Glasgow to form the Alquife Mines & Railway Company Limited in the province of Granada in southern Spain. As a result, ore was obtained cheaply from opencast mines, where conditions were described as 'feudal', via a seven-and-a-half mile branch railway to the port of Almeria. From there it was shipped to the ironworks pier on the banks of the Duddon where five vessels of 500 tons each could be accommodated. Initial expectations were for around 100,000 tons of ore annually from Alquife. In 1925 the M&AHIC became sole owners of the Alquife operation and of the ore loading terminal at Almeria. Output from the company's Spanish mines was far greater than was necessary to supply the Millom works and so ore was sold on the open market; ironically, in the light of world events, the largest percentage went to Germany.

Relationships with the adjacent Hodbarrow company were never entirely convivial and in September 1900, in a further attempt to satisfy the demand for iron ore from its own resources, the M&AHIC reached agreement to purchase the Ullbank royalty, and the Ullbank Mining Company was formed. On 28th September 1903 a branch line was opened to the new mine, leaving the London & North Western and Furness Joint line at Ullcoats Junction, south of Egremont. This junction with the former Whitehaven, Cleator & Egremont Railway also served the adjacent Ullcoats mine branch that had opened on 11th August 1902. The first shaft at Ullcoats was sunk in 1900 and eventually it too fell into the hands of the M&AHIC as it continued to strive for self-sufficiency. The LNWR and FR agreed to build and maintain the Ullbank mine sidings at the expense of the M&AHIC. The latter also agreed to pay for a man to open and shut the gates when the railway companies' locomotives were working at the sidings. In addition, the Millom company paid towards the cost of the new signal box and the signalman's wages and clothing.

The early years of the new century saw a depression in the haematite trade. In 1908 the M&AHIC was reported as having only two of its ten furnaces at work, while the FR's half-yearly meeting in February 1910 reported that the depression of the previous two years, which had affected the railway, was slowly moving away and that three furnaces were then in blast at Millom. The FR Traffic & Works Committee noted at its January 1910 meeting that, although pig iron forwarded from Millom in 1909 was 43,029 tons (almost the same as the previous year), iron ore, coal and coke received by rail was up by 19,958 tons to 256,005 tons. Ore imported through Barrow docks for Millom rose from 10,736 tons in 1908 to 39,876 tons (a massive 271% increase) in 1909. As recently as 1905 the M&AHIC had agreed with the FR to import not less than 150,000 tons of ore through Barrow for its Askam and Millom establishments in the year ending August 1906. In January 1914 the first sod was cut for the new shaft at the second Ullbank pit, and at the company's AGM in November that year the "heaviest discovery of ore in Cumberland in the Company's history" was celebrated. The West Cumberland mines were to keep the Millom furnaces in blast through some difficult times ahead as other ironworks in the area closed down.

The First World War created an artificial, and temporary, demand for iron and steel for ships and munitions, the *acid pig* proving ideal for use in naval armaments and especially in the production of armour plating, but Cumbrian industries as a whole were subsequently to find it difficult to adjust to

47

Millom Ironworks No 13, an Andrew Barclay product built in 1906 as Works No 1054, poses ahead of a Sentinel on 11th June 1961. Formerly North Lonsdale No 5, the 0-4-0ST moved to Millom in 1947/8 just before the Ulverston foundry closed in 1949. The boiler was put on the still-extant No 12 and the remains scrapped in 1969.

Photo: KJ Cooper 1377, Industrial Railway Society copyright

post-war conditions. The M&AHIC used this short period of wartime prosperity to firstly take a controlling interest in the Barrow Hematite Steel Company (BHSC) in 1916 and then in 1917, together with the North Lonsdale Iron & Steel Company (NLI&S) of Ulverston and the BHSC, to purchase the Ullcoats Mining Company. The share split was M&AHIC 3/8, BHSC 3/8 and NLI&S ¼. George Mure Ritchie, a Scottish lawyer who had been chairman of the M&AHIC since 1893, also took over the chair of the BHSC in 1916, the same year that he became a director of the Furness Railway; Ritchie had many more directorships in Whitehaven, South Wales, Yorkshire and Co Durham. During the final year of the War, the BHSC, in conjunction with the M&AHIC, acquired the Camerton Coal & Firebrick Company, thereby securing a supply of firebricks and refractory materials. The pattern for the next fifty years, whereby the ironworks took over their suppliers, was steadily taking shape. By 1918 modern stoves, pig breakers, turbo-blowers, turbo-alternators and a gas cleaning plant had been installed at Millom, but the future of the works on the other side of the estuary was not so secure. Askam Ironworks closed on 19th April 1919, when it was decided to concentrate all the work at Millom, although at the time the company believed that there would be a future for Askam when the vast new deposits in West Cumberland came to be worked at full capacity. Finding themselves with a number of serviceable locomotives at Askam and no work for them, at least four 0-4-0ST and 0-6-0ST locomotives were transferred to the Cumberland side of the Duddon around 1919. Unfortunately, the optimism was unfounded and Askam Ironworks never re-opened, although it was not finally demolished until 1938. Near Egremont, the original Ullbank pit was abandoned in 1919 and what would have been Ullbank No 2, by then named *Florence* after Mrs Mure Ritchie, finally started to produce ore for output in May 1922, the long delay being attributed to the recent hostilities. The FR had already constructed a connecting line from Florence Pit Sidings in 1916 at the M&AHIC's expense and the branch appears to have been worked by M&AHIC locomotives. Most of the locos which worked at Florence came second-hand from other Cumberland sites but all eventually ended up at Millom Ironworks.

Just as the Florence mine was about to prove its worth, the post-war depression began to have a serious effect in the area. *The Times* reported in January 1921 that the Millom Ironworks had been damped out, that Hodbarrow had been closed indefinitely and that nearly the entire working population of the district was unemployed. The massive reduction in the demand for iron and steel was having an appalling effect in an area which was almost totally dependent on a single industry. Nor was the problem confined to Millom: at the FR AGM in March 1922 it was reported that, out of more than 40 blast furnaces in Furness and West Cumberland, there had never been more than eight in blast since August 1921. Nationally, pig iron production had plummeted from 8 million tons in 1920 to 2.5 million tons in 1921. Despite one or two optimistic fluctuations, this state of affairs was to persist locally until the period of national rearmament prior to the advent of the Second World War. After 1921 no dividend was paid on the ordinary Millom and Askam shares until 1938 but, despite the lack of demand for its product, the company was far from idle during this difficult period. It increased its share in the Whitehaven Colliery Company until, by 1928, it was the largest shareholder in that concern. In 1932 the North Lonsdale Iron & Steel Company was merged with the M&AHIC, thereby ensuring total control of the Ullcoats Mining Company, adjacent to the already-owned Florence Mine. Between 1934 and 1939 the Millom works went through a major reconstruction as iron production was concentrated on this site. On the other hand, the Ulverston furnaces were out of blast between October 1931 and April 1937. A sintering plant was installed in 1935, three modern blast furnaces (each capable of producing about 300 tons per day) were constructed, a pig-casting machine built (although sand-cast pigs continued to be produced until 1939) and a large blower was installed from the closed Askam works. The Spanish Civil War halted the supply of ore from the Alquife mines from July 1936 and this, together with the demand for pig iron as a result of the rearmament programme, resulted in the West Cumberland mines working at full production and the M&AHIC continuing to search for more ore reserves. As demand for iron increased prior to the outbreak of war, the company expressed its wish to put the North Lonsdale furnaces into blast but, without the Alquife ore, it was not possible to resume operations at Ulverston at a profit. In 1938 the decision was taken to effect closure, the furnaces being blown out on 15th August. However, the foundry continued to operate, supplied with pig iron from Millom. Ironically, by 1940 ore started to arrive again from Alquife, following the end of the Civil War in April 1939.

Millom Ironworks (1867 - 1968)

On 29th July 1947 Millom No 8, formerly Almeida, hauls a train of ancient wooden wagons through the ironworks site. Built by Andrew Barclay in 1871 as Works No 114, this loco was rebuilt by Lowca Engineering in 1890, again by New Lowca Engineering in 1920 and finally at Millom in 1940. It arrived from Cleator Moor ironworks in the early 1920s and was finally scrapped in 1955.
Photo: AN Glover/Kidderminster Railway Museum

Millom Ironworks No 3, formerly Croft End, shunts a North Eastern Railway coke hopper wagon on the shores of the Duddon on 29th July 1947. No 3 was built by the New Lowca Engineering Company in 1912 as Works No 250 and came to Millom from Florence No 1 mine around 1937. Surviving as late as 1970, the loco was unfortunate in being scrapped on site in May that year.
Photo: AN Glover/Kidderminster Railway Museum

Chapter Four

West Cumberland south of Egremont in the mid 1950s
The Millom & Askam Hematite Iron Company eventually owned all these mines. The branch to Florence No 1 survived for several years after the mine closed in 1948. Florence No 2 was connected to Ullcoats in the 1950s and worked as a combined operation.

Drawn by Alan Johnstone, based on an Ordnance Survey Map.

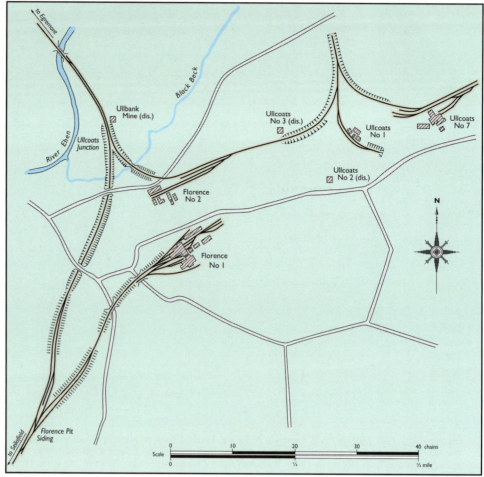

In the same way that the Millom company had closed the Askam ironworks after the First World War, so the North Lonsdale ironworks was shut down after the Second War. The site was sold to Glaxo Pharmaceuticals in January 1947. All iron manufacture had been concentrated at Millom since 1938 and, once the new foundry opened there in September 1949, the Ulverston works closed entirely in November that year. Its own foundry worked at full capacity to the end, latterly supplied with a readily-available quantity of scrap from the demolition of the ironworks. Similarly, just as the sinking of Florence No 1 pit had been delayed by the first global conflict, so Florence No 2 (which had been started in 1940) was not completed until May 1946 and did not raise ore until August 1948. No 1 closed around this time, leaving the branch from Florence Pit Sidings redundant since the new pit was served by sidings from the Ullcoats branch. However, the Florence branch seems to have survived until closure around April 1956.

Shortly after the Second World War, the quarry at Redhills, which had produced limestone since the ironworks opened in 1867, was closed and henceforth supplies were obtained from the Goldmire quarry near Dalton. The long rail connection to Redhills was at one time extremely busy carrying limestone towards the works and slag away from it and it is reported that such was the level of traffic that a form of single line staff working was employed at one time. Up to 1937 slag was tipped at Redhills, after which time a new connection was laid across the Hodbarrow railway to allow the ladles of molten slag to be tipped behind the Outer Barrier. Tipping continued there until August 1952, from which date all tipping took place on the banks of the Duddon, where it built up new ground for future development worksites and stocking areas. Once it ceased to carry slag ladles, the Redhills line was used as a store for condemned and cripple wagons belonging to the ironworks.

This Hudswell Clarke (762 of 1906) 0-4-0ST, Millom No 2 Ethel, worked at Carnforth Ironworks before coming to Millom around 1938. The 20 ton hopper wagon on the right, in this 29th July 1947 picture, was one of a batch of iron ore hoppers ordered from Charles Roberts of Wakefield on 19th January 1937. Ethel succumbed to the torch in 1953.

Photo: AN Glover/Kidderminster Railway Museum

Millom Ironworks (1867 - 1968)

Peckett 939 of 1902 came to Millom Ironworks from Bradford Corporation's Scar House Reservoir construction in 1937. Seen here on 29th July 1947, the 0-6-0ST took the number 4 on coming to Millom and carried the name *Kitchener* until about 1951. Scrapping came in 1953.

Photo: AN Glover/Kidderminster Railway Museum

1950 found the Millom & Askam Hematite Iron Company in a very strong position: rationalisation, modernisation, increased self-sufficiency and the recent war had resulted in an all-time record in blast furnace production and trading profits in 1949. Such was the demand that the company expressed its concern that it was losing men to the Sellafield nuclear plant, then under construction, and could not recruit sufficient replacements. The Goldmire quarry had been mechanised by the erection of new plant and shipments of ore from Alquife were the best (some 204,469 tons during 1949) for many years. However, nationalisation was imminent and from 15th February 1951 the Millom works and associated mines and quarries (but not the Alquife mines, which were sold to M&AHIC shareholders) became part of the Iron & Steel Corporation of Great Britain. The Hodbarrow Mining Company became part of the Corporation at the same time.

In 1955 managers, anxious to reduce the cost of carrying limestone by rail from Goldmire to Millom, sought quotes for an aerial ropeway across the Duddon from quarry to ironworks. In reply, Ropeways Ltd seemed somewhat wide of the mark in costing a two-mile ropeway to convey iron ore to the long-closed Askam Ironworks. The Millom enquiry was obviously serious and a letter returned, explaining that the requirement was for a ropeway to carry 120,000 tons of limestone per annum across the Duddon but that the prices quoted appeared to show no advantage over using the railway. No further correspondence has been located.

Prospecting in West Cumberland was unaffected by nationalisation and in May 1956 the company wrote to British Railways asking them to defer removing the railway track from Rowrah to Marron Junction due to the exploration for ore at Lamplugh. This line had been closed on 3rd May 1954 but was

A spectacular scene of slag tipping by the Duddon estuary. One of the 1950s-built Sentinel locos waits patiently as its fiery load pours from the ladle. Such scenes lit up the night sky over Millom for a century and left enormous mountains of this waste product of the iron making process.
Photo: Bill Myers Collection

51

Chapter Four

Kerr Stuart No 4009 of 1919 arrived at Millom Ironworks from the Barrow Hematite Steel Co just before the Second World War and took MIW number 10, but shortly after this picture was taken on 11th May 1957 it became number 11. 4009 was exchanged for Hodbarrow Peckett 1647 in the mid 1960s but didn't find much use and was scrapped there shortly after the mine closed.
Photo: LR Perkins/Kidderminster Railway Museum

not finally abandoned until 7th November 1960 (and the track was not lifted until 1964); the Millom intervention achieved its objective but workable ore deposits were never found. Tory ideology did not sit comfortably with the nationalised Iron & Steel Corporation and by 1958 the Millom properties were sold to the Millom Hematite Ore & Iron Company Ltd. Included in the sale was the Hodbarrow Mining Company, finally bringing mine and ironworks into the same ownership; how Thomas Barlow-Massicks would have been celebrating! The directors had not been in favour of nationalisation in 1951 and release from government control saw the company in buoyant mood; a booklet of the time says "Millom . . . commands its own local and assured supply of the best possible ore; a powerful and self-contained production plant with all the latest equipment". The somewhat limited facilities at the company pier were bullishly described thus;

Millom Port is situated on the Duddon Estuary, and under the authority of the Company. Vessels up to 1,200 tons cargo, with up to 15 ft draught can be loaded . . . Direct shipping is undertaken to South Wales, the Continent, etc. The Port is equipped with magnet cranes and vessels are turned round within 24 hours. A pilot boat equipped with radio-telephone is operated by the Company, and ships can be contacted up to 75 miles radius.

In 1959 the company's shares were acquired by the Cranleigh Group, which immediately set about the construction of a new furnace capable of producing 5,500 tons of iron per week. When this new furnace went into blast in May 1961 the works could produce up to 7,000 tons each week (ten times its 1870s figure) but the market was already showing signs of depression and men were being laid off. In January 1963 the Cranleigh Group acquired the Barrow ironworks with the express aim of early closure of the Furness plant, this coming on 31st March of that year. Even this was insufficient to stem the tide as the demand for the low phosphorus merchant pig iron produced at Millom for acid open hearth steelmakers (mainly in Sheffield) and for iron foundries across the country continued to decline. Even so, prospecting for haematite in West Cumberland was still going on in 1965, when ore bodies of over a million tons were located in the Egremont area to replace the dwindling supplies from Florence and Ullcoats still being carried by rail to Millom. Optimism was sufficiently high for a new sinter plant, moved from the closed Barrow works, to be commissioned in 1967.

As demand for the Millom product continued to weaken and competition grew from imported pig iron, the company realised that the only way to exploit its substantial iron-making capacity was to develop the production of steel on site. In association with the British Iron & Steel Research Association (BISRA), a pilot plant was set up in which iron was converted to steel by injecting oxygen as it was run off from the furnace. The term *Millspray* was applied to the process of linking the BISRA spray process to the blast furnace runner and casting the steel continuously. Following successful trials, the world's first commercial-scale spray steelmaking plant opened in May 1966 and approval was sought from the Iron & Steel Board to move to large-scale production in September that year. However, after a long period of prevarication, approval was not forthcoming and with Cranleigh Group profits falling badly, the writing was plainly on the wall for iron making in Millom. "Town fights steel ban" was the heading in *The Times* of 22nd February 1967, which reported "5,554 signatures (almost the entire adult population of the town) on the petition handed to Mr (Richard) Marsh, Minister of Power". The minister chose not to intervene and on Friday 13th September 1968, immediately dubbed *Black Friday*, Millom Ironworks closed its doors after over 100 years and 560 employees were put out of work. Robson Davies, the managing director, described the town as "industrially crippled" and told a public meeting that the government or British Steel could have had the ironworks for £1 if they would have kept it open. Before the meeting a thousand people had marched through the town carrying placards claiming "Millom is doomed" and the town was awash with television cameras and reporters portraying a picture of a supposedly dying town. The shutdown had a serious effect on the port of Barrow: during the first seven months of 1969 it imported or exported 70,500 tons of goods, compared with 160,000 tons during the same period in 1968, the last iron ore being imported in July 1968.

Millom Ironworks No 2 was the twin of the better-known and still surviving No 1. Delivered new to Millom from Andrew Barclay in 1953, No 2 passes a mixed line of wagons on the edge of the Duddon estuary. The rolling slopes of Kirkby Moor on the Lancashire side of the river are in stark contrast to the industrial surroundings in the foreground. No 2 was scrapped on site in May 1969.
Photo: Dave Cousins

With the closure of the ironworks, the demise of the Florence mine was inevitable. Florence and Ullcoats had been connected underground during the 1950s and the combined undertaking closed on the same day as the ironworks, the Ullcoats branch being formally closed on 8th March 1970. However, there were still plenty of haematite reserves and in the following year Beckermet Mines (part of the British Steel Corporation) took it over and linked it to their own mine, working it successfully until 3rd October 1980. Yet again the Florence mine refused to die and the Egremont Mining Company was formed by redundant workers who reopened the workings, making it the last deep working iron ore mine in Europe. A heritage centre opened alongside the mine in 1992 and visitors were able to go underground to view the workings, but this operation, and the mine, closed in 2007 due to the cost of pumping water from the workings. British Nuclear Fuels Ltd at Sellafield had previously paid the cost of pumping water from the mine in order to use it for cooling at the nuclear plant but, once BNFL had no further use for it, the high costs of pumping could not be matched by the sale of ore.

Almost 50 different locomotives, including three diesels, are thought to have worked on the Millom Ironworks site during the 100 years it was in operation. Early machines were bought

Stanier Class 5 45134 on the Hodbarrow branch at Millom Ironworks on the SLS/MLS Furness Railtour on 2nd September 1967. Waiting on the pier crossing is Ironworks No 15 Prince John, built by Andrew Barclay as No 1612 in 1918 and ex-Lever Brothers at Port Sunlight in 1959.

Photo: Colour-Rail.com

Chapter Four

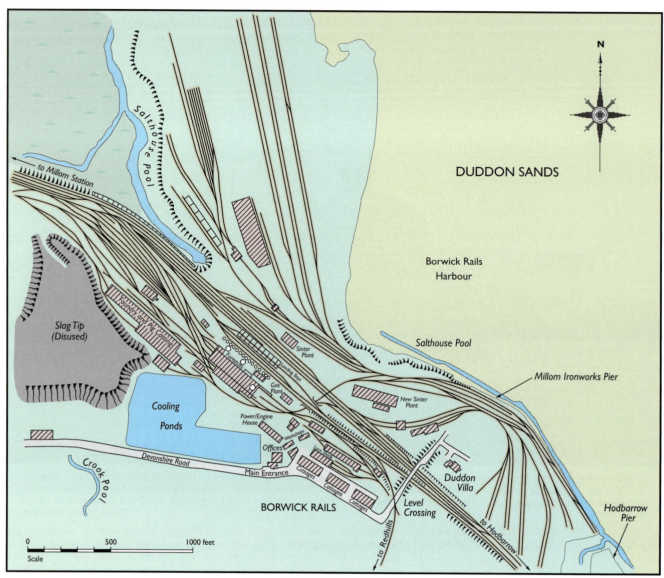

Millom Ironworks in the mid 1960s The works has spread to both sides of the Hodbarrow branch and the tipping of slag on the shores of the estuary has created an enormous area of land for development and storage. The relationship between the two piers can be seen, although the Hodbarrow pier was by then out of use.

Drawn by Alan Johnstone.

new from various manufacturers, but from 1902 until 1953 the company found a ready supply of second-hand locomotives from the various concerns that it had taken over. By the early 1950s some of these were getting rather old and two modern Barclays were ordered, together with four vertical-boilered Sentinels. After 1960 more second-hand locomotives were becoming available at cheap prices and the Millom company took advantage of this. An official Millom Hematite Ore & Iron Company Ltd publication of 1959/60 gives a list of the rolling stock operating on the works' thirty miles of railway (see Table 6). It has been possible to extend this list in order to provide greater details of the locomotive stock at that time (see Table 7). The final arrivals were three Fowler diesel-hydraulics from Barrow Ironworks in 1963. Everyday work at the plant required an extensive fleet and, even as late as 1967, eight locomotives were in daily use.

Following closure, the Fowler diesels went to British Steel Corporation's Workington docks and most of the remaining steam locomotives were scrapped on site but two were fortunate enough to survive into preservation. No 12 led an itinerant existence at Earnse Bay caravan site on Walney, at Carnforth Steamtown, then Haverthwaite and most recently in Gloucestershire, while its more modern sister, No 1, went to Carnforth and then Haverthwaite, where it is currently operable. Particularly unfortunate were No 3, one of very few Lowca-built locomotives then in existence, which was cut up on site in 1970 and No 9, the last surviving inside-cylinder Peckett 0-4-0, which had come from Barrow Steelworks when that establishment was dieselised in 1960 and which was cut up on site as late as 1972. For a period of over two years following closure the

works was dismantled and shipped out in pieces from the pier until finally in July 1970 the last working locomotive, No 1, finished moving scrap. On 11th October the following year Dr Hubert Jackson, who had bought the loco, and Joe Walker, the former ironworks locomotive superintendent, enjoyed the journey of a lifetime on the footplate of the Barclay as it was hauled from Millom to Steamtown at Carnforth in light steam behind English Electric Type 4 (Class 40) No 330. BR's quote of £85 covered "haulage and the provision of a 'caretaker' during the movement over BR lines, subject to the locomotive being passed as fit to run on its own wheels".

After closure the pier was used by a ship breaker, although once dredging stopped it was difficult to get ships sufficiently far up river other than at very high tides, and there were also occasional cargoes of crushed granite from Ghyll Scaur quarry

---

Table 6 Millom Ironworks Rolling Stock 1959/60

30 Ore hoppers	26 Pig iron hoppers
36 Pig iron bogies	59 Sinter wagons
19 Large crates (pig caster)	7 Small crates (foundry)
39 Flat wagons	5 Special scrap hoppers
4 Bolster Wagons	27 Slag ladles (10 tons)
9 Large slag ladles (17 tons)	6 Hot metal ladles
Locomotives	**Cranes**
7 Barclay	2 Grabbing cranes
4 Sentinel	4 Ordinary lifting cranes
1 Avonside	4 Magnet cranes
4 Miscellaneous	

Millom Ironworks (1867 - 1968)

Table 7 Millom Ironworks Locomotives 1959/60

MIW No	Builders	Works No	Built
1	Andrew Barclay Sons & Company	2333	1953
2	Andrew Barclay Sons & Company	2334	1953
3	New Lowca Engineering Company	250	1912
4	Sentinel	9585	1955
5	Sentinel	9586	1955
6	Sentinel	9609	1956
7	Sentinel	9610	1956
8	Andrew Barclay Sons & Company	1867	1925
9	Peckett & Sons	1895	1935
10	Peckett & Sons	1934	1937
11	Kerr Stuart & Company	4009	1919
12	Andrew Barclay Sons & Company	929	1902
13	Andrew Barclay Sons & Company	1054	1906
14	Andrew Barclay Sons & Company	1611	1918
15	Andrew Barclay Sons & Company	1612	1918
Ullbank No 1	Avonside Engine Company	1728	1916

(see Chapter 7). The ironworks site is now the home of a local nature reserve and the slag bank has been decapitated, revealing views across the Duddon which had been denied for a century. The pink stains on the ballast from West Cumberland and Barrow Docks iron ore trains are but a memory. Still remaining is Duddon Villa, the managing director's house, first occupied by Thomas Massicks nearly 150 years ago. Would it be too fanciful to suggest that Massicks' ghost still keeps a watchful eye over the site on the banks of the Duddon where it all started?

Having examined Millom's two iron companies in some detail, the next chapter will take a look at the town that sprang up as a direct consequence of their activities.

On 23rd August 1968, shortly before closure of the works, Millom Ironworks No 1, built by Andrew Barclay (Works No 2333), brings a string of hopper wagons of varying ages in front of the sinter plant. Nos 1 and 2 were the last new conventional steam locomotives to arrive at Millom.
Photo: Peter Holmes

Chapter Four

Millom Ironworks bought four new four-wheel Sentinel vertical boiler locomotives in 1955/6. On the occasion of the SLS/MLS Furness Railtour of 27th August 1961 one of them rounds a typically tight curve in the works.

Photo: Ron Herbert

With the sinter plant in the background, John Fowler diesel hydraulic No 7 (JF 4220012 of 1961) shunts a mixed selection of hopper wagons. Three of these 0-4-0s arrived at Millom from Barrow Ironworks in May 1963, following closure of the Barrow plant. When Millom closed they found further use with the British Steel Corporation at Workington Docks.

Photo: Dave Cousins

Millom Ironworks (1867 - 1968)

Millom No 9 was a Peckett Y Class built in 1935 as Works No 1895 and delivered new to Barrow Steelworks. This locomotive came to Millom on 30th November 1960 with its sister of the same class, Peckett No 1934 built in 1937 and which became Millom No 10. No 10 was cut up on site in 1969 but No 9 survived as the last inside-cylinder Peckett 0-4-0 before being scrapped as late as October 1972.
Photo: Pete Stamper

Following closure, Millom Ironworks No 1 awaits its future. This was the last locomotive to work on the site and was preserved, initially at Carnforth and, since March 1978, at the Lakeside and Haverthwaite Railway. The derelict No 1 furnace forms the backdrop to this picture taken around 1970.
Photo: Pete Stamper

This 1968 aerial view of Millom Ironworks shows the Hodbarrow branch passing straight through the works. Devonshire Road leads from the plant, past the cooling ponds to the town, joining Mainsgate Road to the right of the Hodbarrow 'Company Houses'. The two broad thoroughfares middle right are Market Street and Lonsdale Road, while the old village of Holborn Hill sits astride the high ground beyond the railway.
Photo: Bill Myers Collection

The New Town (1866 onwards)

The influence of the iron companies; the Furness Railway as a land owner; the Local Board makes its mark; the great slump; the impact of the ironworks closure; the Co-operative Movement is shaken.

5

"South of the railway is Newtown, a flat peninsula linked to the mainland of Britain only by the railway bridge."
Norman Nicholson, 'Greater Lakeland'

AS SEEN IN Chapter 3, the 1860s saw the efforts of John Barratt and Nathaniel Caine at Hodbarrow bearing fruit and resulting in the large-scale movement of miners and their families into the area as the fortunes of the mine improved in dramatic fashion. At this time the Cornish tin and lead mines were in danger of being worked out and thousands of miners left Devon and Cornwall in search of employment elsewhere. The long journey to South Cumberland for some was not entirely surprising as Henry Schneider, the previously-mentioned discoverer of the huge Park haematite deposit in Furness in 1851, had business connections with the Cornish tin mining industry. One Cornishman, invited by Barratt to become assistant underground manager, was Thomas Rich who arrived in Millom in 1868. Not untypically, Rich went on to become influential in the development of the town, sitting on the Local Board and eventually becoming a JP and Chairman of the Urban District Council. Those miners from the South West who arrived at Hodbarrow met others from Scotland and Ireland to discover an area sadly lacking in accommodation, and very soon all the available houses in Holborn Hill and Haverigg were full; the 1851 Census shows that there were only 77 inhabited houses in the whole of Millom Below and 51 in Chapel-Sucken, which included Haverigg. By 1864 the mining company realised that a crisis had been reached and William Gradwell, a Barrow builder, responded to its request to build temporary timber and corrugated iron huts for the rapidly-increasing Hodbarrow workforce, by then ten times greater than four years previously.

In 1865, as related in Chapter 4, the Cumberland Iron Mining & Smelting Company had started to build its ironworks on the banks of the Duddon and by 2nd July 1866 the *Ulverston Advertiser* reported that there were "between 800 and 1,000 persons above the ordinary population of the neighbourhood". At first extra buildings were put up at Holborn Hill, which soon lost its rural character, but then Ulverston banker John Satterthwaite and John Poole from the same town, supported by Thomas Massicks from the iron company, conceived the notion of building a new town in the vicinity of the proposed works. The Poor Law Amendment Act of 1834 had resulted in the establishment of local unions of parishes, run by Boards of Guardians. The Bootle Board, which came into being on 12th June 1837 and had two Millom Guardians on its elected Board of 16 members, was primarily concerned with the Bootle Workhouse and was not in a position to plan a new town. Consequently, it was left to the Holborn Hill Building Society to purchase from Lord Lonsdale the badly-drained Rottington estate, which was conveniently available as a single block of land. The Building Society was run by Satterthwaite, Poole, Massicks, William Turner and John Matthews; Turner was a partner in Wadham & Turner, the civil engineers of Barrow who surveyed and laid out the new town, and Matthews was the managing director of the new Millom Brick Company Ltd. The *Whitehaven News* of 3rd May 1866 reported that 30 acres of land had been surveyed, laid out in streets and was being drained and made ready for building. On 28th April 1866 the directors of the Building Society, various railway officials and other influential local men met at the newly-opened Station Hotel to celebrate the inauguration of the new town. In March the *Whitehaven News* had confidently stated that it was to be called *Newhaven* but parties at the Station Hotel suggested *Duddon* or *Port Lonsdale*. As was to become increasingly common, Massicks won the day saying that, since the town had "sprung out" of the works then under construction and which was to be called *Millom Ironworks*, it should be called *Millom*.

Thus, from its very inception, the development of the town was inexorably linked with the fortunes of the ironworks and, in particular, with the hand of Massicks. The W&FJR followed suit and Holborn Hill station was renamed *Millom* on 1st June 1866, little more than a month before the W&FJR itself passed into history. The 1867 opening of the Hodbarrow branch allowed the drainage of some of the land on which the new town was to be built. Construction of the railway embankment between the *Banking Bridge* at the end of Lancashire Road and the ironworks allowed some 51 acres of land to be reclaimed from the Duddon estuary. On the eve of the new town's extraordinary impact on the fortunes of the people of south-west Cumberland, *The Schools Inquiry Commission Northern Division 1869* gives an insight into social conditions at the time and what was expected in the years to come:

Whicham and Millom School is situated in a district which was until lately poor. Since the recent opening of mines in the parish of Millom there is every chance of a large increase in the wealth and numbers of the population. The school is for children of the poorer classes.

Unfortunately, the admirable objectives of the promoters of the new town were somewhat thwarted. Although Wadham & Turner's plan is reflected in the grid pattern of the present town, land was sold off piecemeal and the planned sanitary arrangements were not enforced. The area on which the town was built is virtually at sea level and, in conditions best left to the imagination, outbreaks of typhus, typhoid, dysentery and diarrhoea were reported to the Bootle Guardians in 1866. Writing in September that year, the editor of the *Barrow Herald* commented on the extensive building going on but was surprised to see that it was happening on recently reclaimed land where drainage was impossible, rather than on the high ground of Holborn Hill. For their water supply the earliest inhabitants had to depend on a spring which used to be covered at full tide. Massicks prevailed on the Bootle Guardians to improve the spring but it was still inadequate, and vendors travelled the streets with water carts, selling spring water for a halfpenny a bucket. Nonetheless, building proceeded apace: the first place of worship, the Primitive Methodist Chapel in Holborn Hill, was erected in 1866 (the laying of the foundation stone resulted in a train of 25 carriages arriving from Barrow) after Nathaniel Caine had provided £400 towards it and the Wesleyan Church Hall in Queen Street followed in 1867. Caine was a Baptist but helped finance many Methodist chapels, including the two mentioned and the Temperance Hall (Welsh Calvinistic Methodists) in Mainsgate Road; he also financed Methodist chapels at Hill-in-Millom and Broughton-in-Furness. Many of the incoming miners were from Non-Conformist backgrounds and a plethora of different chapels, including the Bible Christian Methodists in Newton Street, the Plymouth Brethren in Crown Street and the Spiritualists in Holborn Hill, eventually appeared in the town. The influx of Irish miners, many of whom had worked with Barratt at Coniston, necessitated a Roman Catholic chapel and this was built in 1868 on land only recently reclaimed from the estuary and described as "practically worthless, a quagmire without roads".

Property speculation in the new town was now rife and the *Whitehaven News* of 7th October 1869 carried the following:

Mr. Henry Atkinson having now completed the New Road [Devonshire Road] through his property, forming the main road to the Cumberland Iron Mining and Smelting Company's furnaces, is open to treat with

59

Chapter Five

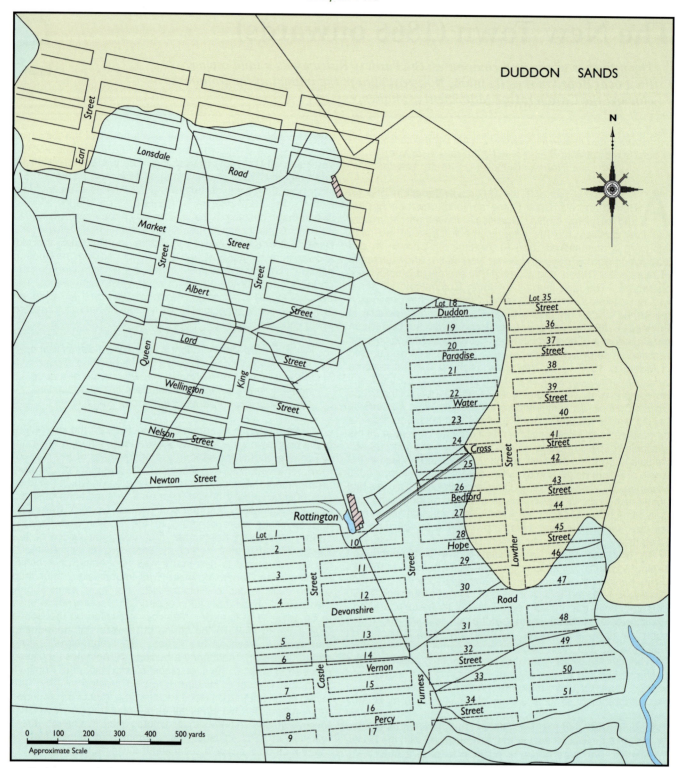

Early proposals for a model town on the Rottington Estate The position of the original coastline shows the extent of the land reclaimed to build the new town. The western street pattern is familiar today but most of the numbered plots further east saw no houses constructed. The only thoroughfares built were Devonshire Road, Furness Street, a short Duddon Street, a tiny Bedford Street, an incomplete Hope Street and the part of Castle Street north of Devonshire Road. The slag bank eventually covered the land east of the proposed Lowther Street and almost reached Furness Street. Nothing was built on the marked plots south of Devonshire Road until a century later, when Wasdale Road and Park Road appeared.

The two large nearly-rectangular plots in the south-western corner of the map were Atkinson's property. Egremont Street was to have been a continuation of Hope Street, Vernon Street would have extended westwards into Brougham Street and Percy Street would have led into Derby Street. Castle Street was planned to extend southwards to Boundary Road (now Boundary Lane) which marked the extent of Atkinson's land. When the Hodbarrow "Company Houses" (Oxford Street, Surrey Street and a third, never constructed) were built on this land, Oxford Street was on the approximate alignment of the proposed Henry Street.

Rottington Cottages now occupy the site of Old Rottington House farm. New Rottington House farm, on the original coastline, was lost under the never-fully-developed eastern end of Lonsdale Road.

Drawn by Alan Johnstone, based on information from Black Combe School and Cumbria Archives.

The New Town (1866 onwards)

This view, looking over Newtown, shows the close proximity of the ironworks to the estuary and its domination of the town, the slag bank almost reaching the oldest terraces. In the centre are the imposing houses in Lapstone Road, following the line of a much earlier route between Lapstone Lodge and the Rottington estate.

Photo: Author's Collection

parties wishing to purchase Building sites. He is confident that his land (Freehold) will be found in all respects best suitable for that purpose, being in a dry situation, easily approached, as well from the Station as from the Furnaces and Harbour, and in close proximity to the recently-discovered Iron Mines.

Atkinson's property consisted of about 20 acres clustered around the junction of Devonshire Road (called *Main Street* on the property map) and Mainsgate Road. Despite the map showing a rectangular grid of streets rejoicing in the names of *Henry*, *Mary*, *Carlisle*, *Derby*, *Castle*, *Brougham* and *Egremont*, only a shortened version of Egremont Street was ever constructed and the only significant building construction on the land was started by the mining company, on a different alignment, 16 years later.

The following decade started ominously with an outbreak of scarlet fever but, more positively, the Holborn Hill Co-operative Society was established in 1870 and the United Methodist Chapel in Newton Street was completed in the following year. Nonetheless, houses were still desperately needed, the population of Millom Below (Newtown and Holborn Hill) having risen from 392 to 2,668 between 1861 and 1871. In 1874 the *Whitehaven Herald* reported "The general condition of Newtown, Millom is a reproach and antithesis to even a remotely approximate sanitary state". Millom was developing without any regulatory control and the Bootle Guardians were powerless to do anything about it. Whilst the ironworks was exerting its influence over Newtown, the mining company preferred to build houses for its workers at Concrete Square in Haverigg and at Steel Green (1872-74). Is it more than coincidence that the newly-built parallel terraces of Newtown pointed directly towards

One of the 19 2-4-0s built for the FR by Sharp, Stewart between 1870 and 1872 draws into Millom's Up platform during the last decade of the nineteenth century. The steps from the original 25ft wide St George's Road bridge can be seen leading down to the platform and the footbridge has yet to be constructed. The Urban District Council later funded the widening of the bridge, the only road access to Newtown.

Photo: Stephe Cove Collection

61

Chapter Five

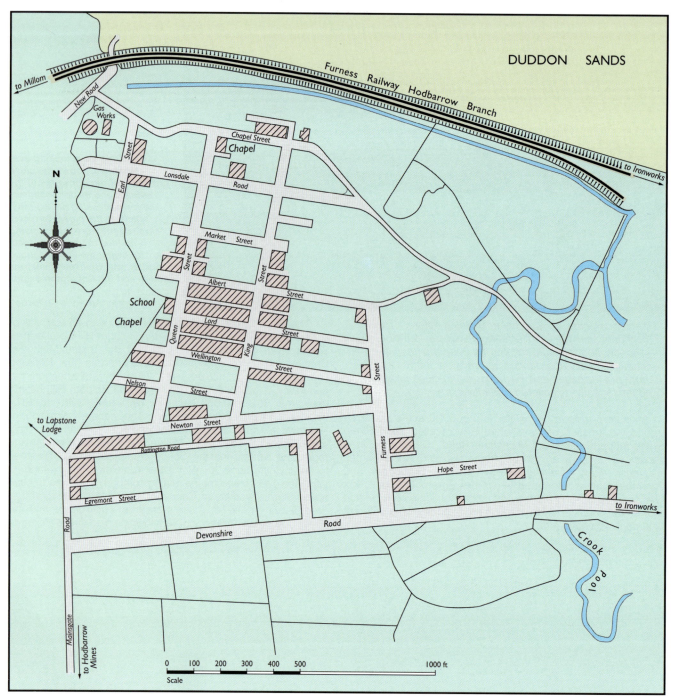

The extent of the new town in 1874 It can be seen how the railway embankment enabled the land to be drained for building purposes. The town centre would move away from Market Street towards the station and the new Market Square in less than ten years.
Drawn by Alan Johnstone, based on information in the National Archives at Kew.

the ironworks? The first houses built were in Albert, Wellington, Nelson and Newton Streets between Queen Street and King Street and towards Furness Street - in other words, that part of the town closest to the ironworks.

Access to the new town from its inception was on the alignment of the old road from the Station Hotel at the bottom of Main Street in Holborn Hill to Lapstone Lodge Farm, which was situated at the junction of the later Lapstone Road and Lancashire Road. Since the arrival of the W&FJR in 1850 a level crossing had taken the road across the railway at the western end of Holborn Hill station but, by the 1870s, the increased amount of road and rail traffic caused Nathaniel Caine (by then a JP) to make repeated applications to the FR for a bridge to replace the crossing. Caine's frustration started a bizarre sequence of events when, in January 1872, he wrote to the Board of Trade pointing out that the growth of the new town south of the crossing, the large numbers employed at the ironworks and at Hodbarrow and the delays caused by trains shunting were resulting in people going to work "passing between trains and under trains". Lieutenant-Colonel Hutchinson RE, from the Board of Trade, inspected

the site in February and, having received his report, the FR, unwilling to build the bridge, wrote back saying that the road crossed on the level was not a turnpike and "leads nowhere except to the New Colony and the Iron Works" but that the directors would give their attention to constructing a footbridge as part of the imminent new station. The railway company subsequently had a change of heart and, by August 1874, had built the bridge, together with inclines, and had closed the crossing. Not everyone was satisfied, however, for later that month solicitors acting for the Bootle Highway Board wrote to the Board of Trade complaining that the FR's closing of public highways was illegal and that those wishing to cross the line now had a greater distance to cover than previously and had to contend with steep inclines; moreover, it was felt that the recent doubling of the track rendered a bridge unnecessary. The Board stated they had not intervened sooner, having mistakenly assumed that the railway company had already acquired the appropriate powers. Again Hutchinson made his way from Whitehall to Cumberland and, while observing that the FR had correctly recognised the danger of the level crossing, he felt they had "committed a grave indiscretion" in closing

The New Town (1866 onwards)

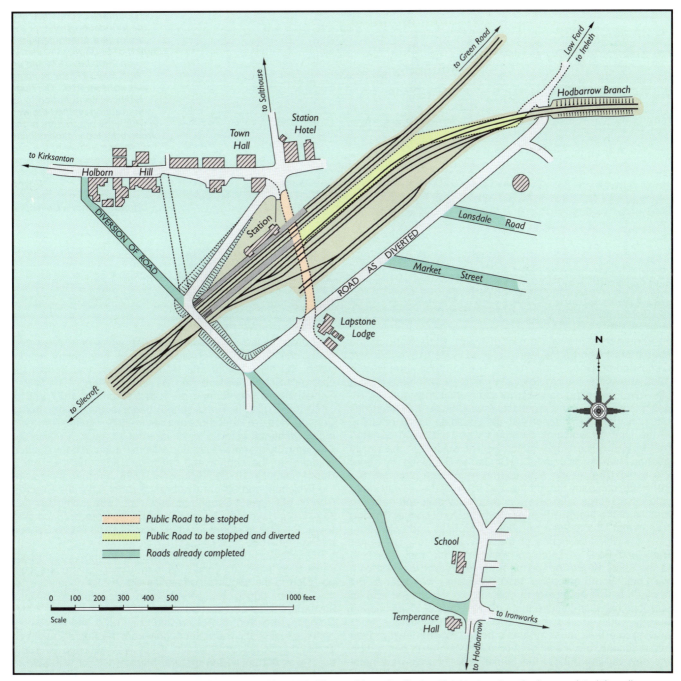

The saga of the level crossing and the bridge 1872-1876 The road from the Station Hotel to Lapstone Lodge pre-dated the railway. Closure of this road enabled the FR to rebuild the station, enlarge the siding space and remodel the branch junction. The railway company was also responsible for much road building around the station.

Drawn by Alan Johnstone, based on information in the National Archives at Kew.

roads without authority. He instructed the railway company to apply to Parliament for the appropriate powers, although he gave a strong hint that the inhabitants of the town would be well advised not to oppose the Bill. The Bill came before Parliament in the 1876 session and the FR gained authority to make the road closures, to build Station Road, St George's Road, the bridge and Lancashire Road and to finish Lonsdale Road and Market Street. Of course, all this had been completed by this time and all the railway company did was to sell off land for house building, construction of the gas works and police station, and to pass over a sum of money to the new Local Board in order to provide flagged pavements. Thus Millom's inhabitants gained improved access to the new town, as well as several major new roads at the FR's expense.

The outbreak of smallpox in 1872 stimulated both the two iron companies and the church to seek to replace the Bootle Guardians with a local authority and, on 5th March 1875, the Millom Local Board of Health was formed, with ironworks representatives forming the majority of its members and, almost inevitably, with Thomas Massicks as its first chairman. The 1870s saw a shift in the town centre: the original plan had been for the appropriately named Lonsdale Road to be the main street, to which end it was laid out to a width of 50ft and, together with Market Street, led to the market on a one-acre site at the eastern end of these broad thoroughfares. By the end of the decade, however, the present Market Square had become the hub of the new town. The shift began at a meeting convened at the ironworks by the increasingly influential Massicks on 10th June 1873 to consider the spiritual needs of the inhabitants of the new town. Among those present were Massicks and George Horsfall from the ironworks, the Bishop of Carlisle and Sir James Ramsden (Managing Director of the Furness Railway and Barrow's first Mayor), together with Nathaniel Caine and Cedric Vaughan (both from Hodbarrow). Despite the presence of the last two, the mining company took no further part and it was Massicks who insisted that finely-dressed stone was used for the planned new church and ensured that the ironworks directors contributed over £8,000 out of a total cost of £13,465 (nearly five times the cost of the Wesleyan Chapel in Queen Street built at the same time). The mining company contributed £1,000. Designed in the Gothic style by Lancaster architects Paley and Austin and built in red

Chapter Five

The Countess of Lonsdale laid the foundation stone for the Paley and Austin-designed church of St George the Martyr on 29th July 1874 and on 28th May 1877 the building was consecrated. The huge financial contribution to its construction typified the way in which the proprietors of the ironworks took responsibility for the welfare of the new town's population in the days before the creation of the Local Board.

Photo: Author's Collection

St Bees sandstone with a roof of Kirkby slate, work on the church of St George the Martyr started in May 1874 and was completed on Good Friday 1877. The tip of the spire is over 130ft above the 70ft high glacial drumlin on which the church sits, overlooking the new railway station buildings of 1872-76, designed by the same architects (see Chapter 6). Massicks had considerable influence with the Lonsdale family, resulting in the land on which St George's was built being donated by the Earl. The single stained glass window in the newly opened church was paid for by Sir James Ramsden. At about the same time as the new church was being planned, the ironworks company bought the land south of the railway, up to where St George's Terrace was eventually built and between the site of the proposed church and Lapstone Lodge. Having taken what was needed for church purposes and sold some plots on which branches of the York City Bank, Lancaster Bank and Bank of Liverpool were built, the rest was sold to the Local Board for use as a market, which opened with the Local Board offices in 1879. Massicks was later to tell his friends that his object in opening out the market and its surroundings was to keep it out of the hands of a speculating builder. Just as the town's two dominant industries were moving into their most profitable period, so the town moved into a second, more confident phase of its growth centred on the new railway bridge, the Market Hall, church, new hotel and public buildings.

Following the 1870 Education Act, which laid down that every child had to be provided with an elementary school place, the New Millom and Hodbarrow National School (St George's School) was opened in Lapstone Road. The Millom School Board was formed on 10th September 1877 and in 1878 the Lapstone Road school became the Millom Board School. Holborn Hill School opened in 1879; like the Newtown establishment it catered for children of all ages. Prior to the Act some children had attended Millom Parish School, opened adjacent to the church and castle in 1858; this became a Board School in 1878 and closed in 1886. Further afield were the Whicham and Millom Grammar School (later the Silecroft Church of England School), dating from 1689 (some sources say 1540), Haverigg Church School dating from 1875 (coming under the Millom Board in 1879) and The Hill Board School, dating from 1883.

Only towards the end of the 1870s did the new Local Board succeed in improving conditions in the town, but credit should be given to the two iron companies which had negotiated for the powers during the period when the Bootle Guardians had supposedly had responsibility: the Millom Gas & Water Company received its Act on 2nd July 1875, the gas works opening that year. The water supply from the Board's reservoir at Baystone Bank in Whicham Valley was obtained by 1880, but it was not until 1885 that the Medical Officer was able to comment favourably on sanitary conditions in the town. Some

The Market Square with the West County Hotel, market and Local Board offices dates from 1879, by which time this was the undisputed Millom town centre. The market closed during the Second World War and later found use as a pyjama factory, while the clock tower looks rather less elegant these days, having been reduced in height.

Photo: Author's Collection

64

The New Town (1866 onwards)

The Cambridge Hotel stands at the corner of Duke Street and Cambridge Street on land formerly owned by the Furness Railway. This 1880s view shows something of the unfinished nature of parts of the town at that time, an issue that caused the Bulmer's Directory of the period to comment that 'a great deal yet remains to be accomplished'. Some of the pre-nineteenth century properties of Holborn Hill village are seen on the far right.
Photo: Stephe Cove Collection

idea of the problems faced by the Bootle Board of Guardians, the iron companies and eventually the Local Board can be gleaned from the growth in the combined population of Millom Above and Millom Below from 900 in 1861 to 3,272 ten years later and to 7,698 by 1881.

Throughout the 1880s the town gained in maturity and its reputation as something of a "Wild West" outpost began to fade, although Bulmer's *1883 History and Directory of West Cumberland* unflatteringly describes Millom as:

> ... still in a very unfinished state; large patches of vacant ground greatly disfigure its appearance and the streets seem at the commencement to have been plotted out without any ultimate design. The Local Board, since its establishment, has done much to improve the town, but a great deal yet remains to be accomplished.

The Hodbarrow *Company Houses* in Oxford and Surrey Streets, built parallel to Mainsgate Road, the main route to the mine and which had originally led to the shore, appeared between 1885 and 1889. Our Lady and St James church was erected in 1888, funded by deductions from the wages of Catholic miners. Further accommodation for Non-Conformist worshippers was completed in 1884 in the form of the Baptist Chapel in Crown Street and the 1889 erection of the Salvation Army Citadel in Nelson Street virtually completed a full set of places of worship. Building in Albert Street and Wellington Street continued to spread westwards until, in 1888, the completion of the Co-operative buildings, containing shops and a public hall, confirmed the top end of Wellington Street as Millom's main shopping area. Just as the town's future prosperity was inexorably linked with the fortunes of the iron making and mining companies, so was the success of the Millom Co-operative

This postcard view from St George's church tower dates from between 1902, when the station footbridge was erected, and the start of work on the Up platform awning in 1907. A train of Furness six wheel and bogie carriages awaits departure for Barrow and the goods yard is packed with traffic. Prominent in the right foreground is the West County Hotel and in the centre is the goods shed, now converted to a supermarket.

Photo: Bill Myers Collection

Chapter Five

HOLBORN HILL, MILLOM, FROM THE CHURCH TOWER.

St George's vicarage is in the foreground and the original small turntable sits opposite the signal box destroyed in 1913. Holborn Hill School is in the centre of the picture and the open ground between it and the railway would house the Palladium by 1912. The war memorial was erected on the space in front of the Masonic Hall on the extreme right and high status housing can be seen to the north of Holborn Hill.
Photo: Author's Collection

Society, renamed from the Holborn Hill Co-operative in 1887, part of this dependency. The Co-operative movement had grown rapidly among the iron mining communities in Victorian Cumberland and, although the Millom Society's growth was not as spectacular as that in Cleator Moor, it was to grow from just 341 members of the Holborn Hill Society in 1875 to 1,007 eleven years later. By 1910 there were branches in Albert Street, Holborn Hill, Haverigg and Bootle. The catastrophic events of 1969 were still more than half a century in the future.

The town continued to prosper throughout the 'nineties; the Local Board showed some foresight in 1891 by buying the failed Millom Club and Institute and converting it into the town's library, reading room and Science, Art and Technical School. The Board itself, through an Act of 18th June 1894, became the Millom Urban District Council and the two townships of Millom Urban District (comprising the wards of Newtown North, Newtown South, Holborn Hill and Haverigg) and Millom Rural were formed. The same Act created Bootle Rural District Council, which eventually amalgamated with Millom UDC in 1934 to form Millom Rural District Council. At the time of its creation, Millom Rural District contained the civil parishes of Bootle, Drigg & Carleton, Eskdale, Irton, Millom, Millom Without, Muncaster, Seascale, Ulpha, Waberthwaite and Whicham; an enormous area of some 89,000 acres which was even bigger than the old Millom Parish and the original Lordship of Millom. Houses and public buildings continued to be constructed throughout the 1890s: the Police Station (replacing an earlier building in Salthouse Road), Conservative Club and the banks all belong to this period, but with the building of the Recreation Hall (later Palladium) in 1912, most of the town's construction was finished and further significant developments would not be seen until after the Second World War. Table 8 shows how the population of Millom Civil Parish changed between 1881 and 1931: the 1901 figure was inflated due to the large number of men working on the Outer Barrier at Hodbarrow.

The period of prosperity enjoyed by the mine and the ironworks during the 1914-18 War came to an abrupt end once peace was restored: the same was true of the town they had spawned. The Depression of the 1920s and 1930s found West Cumberland and Furness particularly vulnerable, as these areas were largely dependent on the manufacture of iron. Maryport, Cleator Moor and Millom were described at the time as being, or threatening to become, 'industrially derelict'. In order to create employment in the hard-hit town, the Urban District Council announced plans in 1922 for the construction of three road schemes (although these were never implemented) and free meals were made available for children of unemployed men. In his autobiographical *Wednesday Early Closing*, Millom poet Norman Nicholson describes his home town in 1927/29 as "a town abandoned by the industry which had yanked it into being, [where] huge heaps of unsold ore lay beside the shafts at Hodbarrow and, at the iron works, the unsold pig-iron was stacked like enormous, dirty, grey bamboo huts". Nicholson continued by describing the plight of the townsfolk, "a dull smother of hopelessness hung over the town like the smutch from a smoking rubbish dump," and finally, "sheer poverty had hit the people of Millom".

One of Millom's famous sons returned to the town on 23rd May 1925 to unveil the war memorial to the 213 local men who had lost their lives during the War; Major-General Sir Louis Vaughan (1875-1942) was the son of Hodbarrow's Cedric Vaughan and had a distinguished Army career before, during and after the worldwide conflict. The memorial, opposite the railway station (it had been proposed to site it in the Market Square), was designed by Ulverston architect John Brundrit and sculptor Alec Miller of Chipping Campden. Two years later, on 29th June 1927, as the Depression was hitting Cumberland particularly hard, the town had a morale-boosting, albeit brief, visit from the Prince of Wales as he drove up the Cumbrian coast after a tour of the Vickers shipyard at Barrow. In 1928 the Bootle Guardians, in an attempt to provide work, agreed that Millom men could work in the Ghyll Scaur quarry for 44 hours a week in return for 4s 6d (22½p) in cash and the same amount in food vouchers. Table 8 shows that many left the town in search of employment during the 1920s.

Table 8. Population of Millom Civil Parish (figures from Enumeration Returns)

1881	1891	1901	1911	1921	1931
7,698	8,895	10,426	8,612	8,708	7,405

The New Town (1866 onwards)

On 28th March 1968 Millom Ironworks was still in production and its familiar features peer over the slag bank at the foot of Albert Street. An unfamiliar visitor to the yard is brand-new English Electric Class 50, D400, on a crew-training run from Carnforth and, having run round its stock, it prepares to return. Apart from the locomotive and rolling stock, this scene had changed little in 80 years. *Photo: Author*

West Cumberland and Furness did not fully share in the pre-Second World War national recovery due to the large amount of heavy industry in the area and, even as late as 1937, some 30% of the insured population of West Cumberland were still out of work. In 1934 the government passed the Special Areas Act which identified West Cumberland, as well as South Wales, Tyneside and Scotland, as Special Areas with acute employment problems and decreasing populations due to migration, increasing death rates and falling birth rates. Projects aimed at reducing the numbers out of work were funded but the level of investment was not high and firms were reluctant to set up in the Special Areas, with Cumberland faring worse than the others. It was not until 1938, as the national re-armament programme entered its third year, that industry in the area started to revive. The West Cumberland Development Council was constituted in September 1935 under the aegis of the Commissioner for the Special Areas, the first project of the Council being the building of the tannery near Haverigg. Started by Hungarians, Andrew Vigodny and Bruno Herdan, the West Coast Chrome Tanning Company Ltd was incorporated in 1937 and commenced operation at the end of 1938. In May 1938 the Council announced plans for a new silk weaving factory in Whitehaven which would have gone to Millom had the district been able to provide sufficient female workers. During the thirties it was felt in some quarters that the lack of road access to the area was impeding its industrial development, but the Ministry of Transport retorted that, during a 1931 census at Duddon Bridge, only 348 vehicles crossed in a day and so concluded that a new road was unnecessary. In a piece entitled *The Plight of South Cumberland*, *The Times* of 22nd August 1936 supported the notion of a Duddon crossing and made reference to "the miserable train service that crawls from Ulverston to Whitehaven". The desirability of a Duddon barrage was again raised locally and nationally, but its success was once more linked to the building of a Morecambe Bay crossing. Since the latter was unlikely, no further progress could be made on the shorter Duddon crossing; this conclusion had been drawn many years previously and would be again in the future.

The advent of hostilities in 1939 found Millom once more enjoying full employment as local industry worked hard to keep up with the demand for iron and steel. Those who felt that the area was safe from enemy action had their illusions shattered when, on 2nd January 1941, bombs were dropped on Steel Green, destroying three houses and killing five people. Days later two 2,300lb bombs were dropped at Haverigg but missed housing and caused no casualties. Thankfully, these were to be the only such actions for the duration of the War. RAF Millom opened at Haverigg on 20th January 1941 as No 2 Bombing and Gunnery School and, in the following year, became No 2 Observer Advanced Flying Unit. By 2nd January 1945 all flying at Haverigg had ceased and the RAF finally left in 1953. A little-known piece of Millom's railway history was constructed in 1941 in the shape of a moving target range to the south of the airfield. This consisted of a small railway track around which an electrically powered wooden model of an aircraft travelled while gunnery pupils practised firing at it from an aircraft turret. One casualty of the wartime period was the market hall, which was closed in 1942 due to rising losses. In the following year Thomas Nesbitt Ltd opened a factory in Millom after being bombed out in Manchester. Specialising in manufacturing children's nightwear, they eventually had one factory in the old market hall and another in Holborn Hill. Even before the War was over the shortage of housing in the area was appreciated by the Rural District Council and building of the first council houses in Millom was begun at Grammerscroft in 1944. During the next ten years the Council was to build 273 dwellings and the North East Housing Association (a product of the Special Areas programme) built a further 244; by 1968 the 4,730 inhabited dwellings in the Rural District would include 750 let by the RDC.

Reflecting the national situation, post-war recovery was not rapid, although the Development Council did manage to support the opening of A Hearfield & Company's nylon stocking factory in 1949 (merged with Elbeo in 1959) in a small attempt to encourage diversification in an area still dependent on the iron industry. During the 1950s the numbers employed at Hodbarrow fell to a fraction of their levels in the glory days of half a century previously, the 1950 returns showing 248 in total, compared with 1,435 in 1896. By the end of the decade, the ironworks was laying men off and so the numbers travelling out of town to work steadily increased; large numbers travelled daily to Sellafield, Vickers Shipbuilders & Engineers at Barrow, and the Glaxo pharmaceutical plant at Ulverston (opened in 1948).

As late as 1965 *The Times* was still reporting on barrages across the Duddon estuary and Morecambe Bay: the newspaper rightly assumed that the decision to take the M6 over Shap before a final decision was taken on the Bay scheme implied that the latter was doomed. Despite this, hope was still held for the possibility of reclaiming 1,200 acres of the Duddon Sands: more than a century after Stephenson's original scheme, nothing had happened. After being used by the army during the 1950s, the site of RAF Millom was proposed for conversion to a prison during 1967. That, out of the four sites proposed by the Home Office for such conversions, only Haverigg went unopposed says much for the worsening employment picture in the area at the time. Then in 1968 came the not-unexpected closure of Hodbarrow and, more surprisingly, the ironworks. Millom Ironworks had outlasted all its contemporaries in Furness but its closure had a devastating effect, with a quarter of the working population out of work. Consequently the town was designated a Special Development Area by the government. Few eventually stayed "on the dole" but men had to be satisfied with whatever jobs were on offer, with the "aristocrats of their industry", the blast furnace men, becoming labourers overnight. Worse was to come during 1969 when, following a run of shareholders withdrawing their investment capital as a consequence of the ironworks closure, Millom's 2,800-member Co-operative Society suspended withdrawals and was later liquidated. Many Millom men lost their redundancy money which they had invested in the Co-op. The implications of this were felt right across the Co-operative movement when the BBC's *Nationwide* programme featured the plight of the Millom Society, precipitating an unprecedented rush among the Co-operative's 13 million members across the country to withdraw their savings. Within 48 hours of broadcasting £28 million had been withdrawn by savers, with share capital across the movement falling by 9% in the year following the Millom collapse. At the end of 1970 the Co-operative Building Society dropped out of the Co-operative Union and, somewhat ironically, changed its name to the *Nationwide*: the little Cumbrian town had made its name known across the country.

The closure of the ironworks and Hodbarrow mines had left over a square mile of land lying idle, disfigured and with no obvious new use. The 600 acre ironworks site was bought by Millom Investments in 1971 with a view to introducing industrial activity and building a holiday site, but these bold plans were to remain unfulfilled. Once more Millom was designated a Special Development Area by the Board of Trade and government support enabled Drum Closures Ltd to move from Heathrow into the last remaining ironworks buildings in 1969, Sealand Hovercraft to occupy new premises in Devonshire Road in 1971 and new factories making shoes and leather goods to be created.

By the end of the decade, and despite significant government support for new industry, some 1,000 men were estimated to be travelling to Windscale (Sellafield) and Vickers in Barrow. Speaking in 1975, Councillor Peter Cross hit the nail on the head when he said that the main aim must be to alter Millom's image. *The Times* on 20th June 1977 reported that unemployment in the town was running at 11.7% and that if West Coast Tanneries, then in the hands of the receivers, were to close this would rise to 19%, the worst in England. Government assistance was given to the Garston Tanning Company to acquire the tannery but this was only a stay of execution. In June 1979 dismissal notices were issued to signify the end of an enterprise that had started so promisingly in another time of recession 40 years earlier.

The next chapter covers the history of the railway in the years after the Furness Railway took over the Whitehaven & Furness Junction company.

The Co-operative Hall and shops, completed on a prime site at the top of Wellington Street in the previous year, stand ready to open on what appears to be Monday 22nd July 1889. This was Millom's main shopping street and the sturdy Co-op building would no doubt convince its shareholders of the Society's prosperity. This confidence was to be irrevocably shattered in 1969.

Photo: Stephe Cove Collection

The Furness Railway takes over (1866-1923) 6

The Duddon viaduct saga continues; rebuilding the W&FJR; stations and signalling; developments at Eskmeals; the First World War; passenger and freight operations.

"It was resolved that the Duddon Crossing be abandoned and that the Solicitors be instructed to take the necessary steps for applying to Parliament for power to abandon it."
Furness Railway Directors' Minutes 27th October 1868

THE END of Chapter 2 saw how the Furness Railway's purchase of the Whitehaven & Furness Junction Railway was formalised in the Act of 1866. Costing between £10,000 and £14,000 per mile (the national figure was around £20,000 at the time), the W&FJR had been built very cheaply. Not only did the FR inherit 35 miles of single track line laid with iron rails but also the ageing and oft-repaired wooden viaducts at Calder, Drigg, Ravenglass, Eskmeals and Foxfield: the latter two had been provided with "shut off steam" boards to limit speeds as far back as 1858 and by 1860 both had been strengthened with iron rods. To be strictly accurate, in the last year of the W&FJR's separate existence, James Ramsden had suggested that the permanent way needed upgrading with steel rails but the W&FJR Board had only felt able to instigate laying a mile of such track at Holborn Hill. In any case the track would need to be doubled, the viaducts rebuilt in masonry and iron for double track and the primitive stations renewed. Even more significantly, the FR had inherited the obligation to build the Duddon viaduct on the W&FJR alignment. At its meeting on 25th May 1866 the FR Board instructed its engineers to proceed with the renewal of the viaducts at Eskmeals, Ravenglass and Drigg. The Esk viaduct was rebuilt with stone piers during the winter of 1866-7 and the wrought iron girders completed at the end of the year, while Ravenglass and Drigg were similarly reconstructed and completed by June 1868. Interestingly, the contract for the three viaducts had gone to Solomon Woodall of Netherton, near Dudley, and it was agreed that the work would be concluded by the end of July 1867, practically a year sooner than actually happened. The FR Board judged that, since the iron ore traffic was booming and the price of iron was low, it was an appropriate time to build the Duddon viaduct, and, on 9th February 1867, a £29,736 contract was let. PD Bennett & Company were the successful bidders and cast iron components for the viaduct's construction were assembled near Dunnerholme on the Lancashire side of the river. In April 1866 the FR directors had noted that 140,000 tons of Hodbarrow haematite were being shipped annually from Borwick Rails, and they hoped that this would be carried on their new viaduct.

The first part of the scheme to be completed was Railway Number 2 in the 1865 Act - in other words, the Hodbarrow branch. The building of this short (1 mile 75 chain) line was not without drama, the *Whitehaven News* of 12th July 1866 reporting "alarming riots at Haverigg, Millom". There had been a great influx of Irish labourers employed at the Hodbarrow mines and more recently "the deviation line or railway across the Duddon [had] commenced and a great number of navvies belonging to Lancashire and Yorkshire as well as Ireland [had] found employment". Something like 1,000 workmen had been added to the community and most were living at Haverigg. Fighting between the English and Irish seems to have been endemic but on Saturday 30th June the level of violence escalated and the mob attacked, and attempted to drown, PC Caseley from Holborn Hill. The rioting continued through Sunday, when the Harbour Hotel was badly damaged, and into Monday when police from Bootle arrived. It wasn't until more than 30 Whitehaven constables, armed with cutlasses, arrived by train on Thursday that matters eventually were brought under control.

Opened in 1867, the branch ended alongside the Hodbarrow narrow gauge line from the mine to the pier and also served the ironworks, opened in the same year. However, by then the iron trade was suffering one of its periodic depressions, resulting in the Furness directors deciding to defer all work in progress on their system. Consequently, in November construction of the viaduct was suspended, leaving sections of the ironwork on the shore of the estuary. Mindful of the financial strain imposed by renewals elsewhere, by the recent trade depression and perhaps preferring to focus on the development of Barrow and its docks, the FR directors were, in May 1868, voicing their doubts about the immediate need for the Duddon crossing. In September the Board requested Messrs McClean and Stileman, the Railway's consulting engineers, to provide information to enable the directors to decide between applying for powers to abandon the viaduct scheme and seeking a two-year extension. In their report, received by the Board on 27th October, the two engineers estimated that the viaduct would cost £75,000, whilst doubling the line from Millom to Ireleth and reconstructing the Foxfield viaduct would cost around £42,000. Despite a potential saving of 30,000 train-miles per annum, the Coniston traffic would need to be continued and so they estimated a saving of only £750 a year in working costs, adding

Having taken over the W&FJR, the Furness Railway set about doubling the original single track and replacing many of the old wooden station buildings with more substantial stone-built structures. Bootle is a Paley and Austin design, repeated at Drigg, Ravenglass, Greenodd and Haverthwaite. The year of its construction, 1873, is clearly seen on the rainwater head. Photo: Author

69

that the whole of the old line would need to be retained. They reported that the bulk of the Hodbarrow output went by sea to South Wales and Runcorn and that the potential reduction in rates, estimated at 3d (1¼p) per ton, would be insufficient to attract additional business. They considered that shortening the route would have a minimal effect on existing traffic flows and that, when the loss of the mileage proportion of the rates was added to the above, the company would need to find an additional £10,000 per annum, equivalent to 150,000 tons of ore. Faced with such a clear-cut case, the directors took the inevitable decision and, on 9th August 1869, an Act was obtained to abandon the proposed railway across the estuary beyond its junction with the Hodbarrow branch. The House of Lords Select Committee's amendments to the Bill included some good news for Millom and Askam residents and rather less welcome news for the FR. The Furness Railway Act 1869 contains the following:

> Notwithstanding the abandonment of the railway hereby authorized, it shall not be lawful for the company to charge in respect of passenger and goods traffic arising at and conveyed between Askam and Ireleth stations on the south side of the Duddon Estuary and Millom and Hodbarrow stations on the north side of the said estuary any larger amount of tolls and charges than they would have been entitled to demand and receive if the railway across the estuary was completed and opened to traffic.

The distance over the existing line between the two places was six and a half miles, more than double that over the projected viaduct, and passengers from Millom to Barrow soon learned to buy a ticket to Askam and rebook there. The reference to goods traffic in the committee's amendments was to ensure that Hodbarrow to Askam ore rates were kept artificially low to recompense the Furness Iron & Steel Company which could have enjoyed cheaper haulage of iron ore from Cumberland to its Askam ironworks had the viaduct been built.

The £7,500 worth of cast iron components lying at Ireleth were not, however, wasted. When the original wooden Foxfield viaduct was replaced in 1871-2 the contractor, John Gibson, used them for the columns, stanchions, cross heads and longitudinal girders in the new structure. As early as June 1861 the W&FJR Board had received a report saying that the wooden viaduct would need to be rebuilt in three or four years' time and so it must have been in a very poor condition ten years later. Gibson also used some of the redundant metalwork in the reconstruction of the wooden viaducts across Kirkby Pool and over the Calder at Sellafield. The new Foxfield viaduct, comprising 13 spans of 25ft each, was some 400 yards shorter than its predecessor, the difference resulting from construction of a solid embankment. At least the material assembled for the Duddon crossing was eventually used for its intended purpose, even if this was four miles further upstream. This link with the ill-fated Duddon crossing survived until 1921 when the FR replaced the iron viaduct with the present steel, concrete and brick structure, made up of four 50ft spans and a central span of 75ft. This viaduct was refurbished by Stobart Rail in 2011. The crossing of the Duddon continued to engage the interest of the local press. Thirteen years after the passing of the Act abandoning the railway across the estuary, the *Lancaster Gazette* carried a report on the FR's opening of the Barrow loop line on 1st June 1882, adding "It is anticipated that the estuary of the Duddon will, at no distant date, be crossed by a bridge and thus shorten the distance from Barrow to Whitehaven by about ten miles". As a postscript to the Duddon viaduct saga, evidence suggests that some of the columns salvaged from the 1867 viaduct materials and subsequently used by Gibson at Foxfield, may have had a third use in supporting the platform extension over the road bridge just north of Ravenglass station. The columns certainly look similar and the dates are consistent.

The opening of the line from Egremont to Sellafield (controlled by the Cleator & Furness Railway Committee) on 1st August 1869 provided an outlet to the south from the haematite mines of West Cumberland, with the result that traffic on the

Foxfield viaduct was built by the FR in 1871-2 using some of the columns, stanchions, longitudinal girders and cross heads from the 1867 Duddon crossing scheme. This structure survived until rebuilt in 1921 but some of the ironwork from the 1867 scheme may still exist at Ravenglass station.
Photo: CRA Library Ref WKR006

The Furness Railway takes over (1866 - 1923)

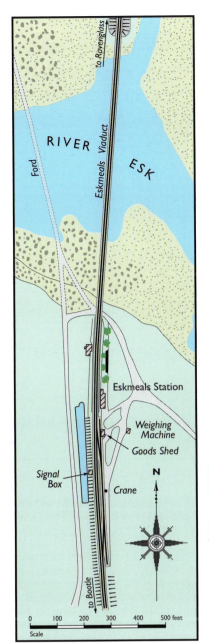

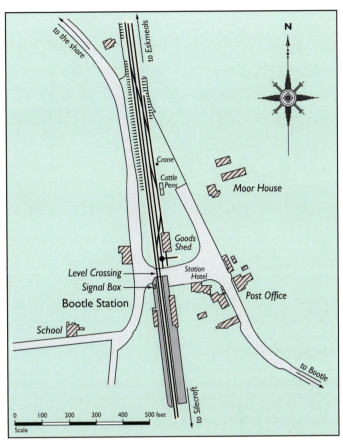

Left - Eskmeals Station circa 1900 Other than the double track, the FR replacement station offered little more in the way of facilities than its W&FJR predecessor. Only the proximity of the Gun Range kept it open for so long as there was little traffic offering from the sparsely populated hinterland.

Above - Bootle Station circa 1900 The distance of the station from the village led to the formation of a separate community, Bootle Station, with its own bank and post office. The wagon turntable at the south end of the goods shed is worthy of note.

Station plans drawn by Alan Johnstone and are based on maps in the CRA Collection.

single track coastal route continued to grow rapidly. Some idea of the problems associated with working goods traffic at the time can be gleaned from a Board of Trade report into an accident at Millom on 9th August 1871. A mineral train from Whitehaven, comprising two engines, 84 wagons and brake van, was held at signals when it was struck in the rear by a passenger train of five vehicles and a brake van. The enquiry put the blame primarily on the station master for not having sent a man out to act as an:

unmistakable distant signal when he saw that the fixed one was not acting properly and when there was a train hidden by the curve in the line only 390 yards inside it; and, secondly in giving 'line clear' to Silecroft, certainly contrary to the printed instructions as to block-telegraph working.

The station master claimed the volume of traffic at the station was such that it could not be worked if he adhered strictly to the rules and the inspector noted that "alterations are now in progress at Millom which will give more siding accommodation from want of which the station is now suffering." The replacement of the road from the Newtown side of the level crossing to the Duddon ford by Lancashire Road in 1874 (see Chapter 5) released sufficient additional land to build these sidings and the branch junction was moved from behind the Station Hotel to the west of the new road bridge.

FR dividends between 1870 and 1873 averaged a very healthy 9½% but then collapsed due to the fall in demand for, and the price of, iron and steel and the much derided, by shareholders and the local press, expenditure on the docks at Barrow. Dividends never again approached the dizzy heights of 10% during the company's lifetime, the *Lancaster Gazette* in March 1875 laying the blame squarely on the expansion of the docks:

The dividends of [the shareholders] and the comfort of [the general public] have been sacrificed of late on the shrine of Dock manias by the short-sighted policy of the Directors.

During the early 1870s the FR continued the virtual rebuilding of its Foxfield to Whitehaven acquisition. Conversion to double track was a priority; the contractor James C Hunter completed Seascale to Bootle by April 1872, Foxfield to Millom by March 1873, Millom to Bootle by December 1873 and finally Seascale to Sellafield by July 1874, following the completion of the Calder viaduct in 1873. In August 1873 the FR chairman told the half-yearly meeting that "increased traffic [had] rendered it desirable to double a larger portion of the line than the directors originally anticipated" but within two years all was to change. To complement the double track alignment, the company commenced a programme of rebuilding the W&FJR wooden station structures either in stone or by providing wooden replacements in its familiar "Swiss chalet" style. The Duke of Devonshire, speaking to FR shareholders in 1875, explained the problem of the W&FJR buildings:

Chapter Six

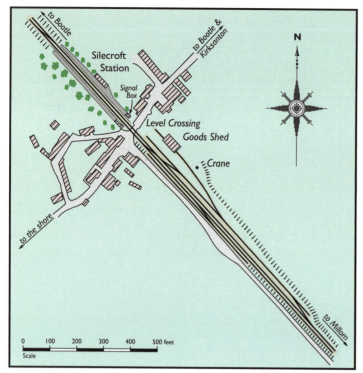

Above - **Silecroft Station circa 1900** Whilst the village has expanded little in 40 years, the goods facilities are a big improvement on those the FR inherited from the W&FJR. Note the signal box in its pre-1924 position on the opposite side of the crossing.

Right - **Green Road Station circa 1900** The lack of business at this remote station caused it to be proposed for closure on two occasions other than in the Beeching report.

On the Whitehaven section especially some of the stations were of a most inferior description and such as the Board of Trade would not have them continue. They were temporary structures scarcely more than wooden hovels and it was absolutely necessary to lay out a good deal of money in improving them.

At Eskmeals the Up platform received a typical FR rustic wooden waiting room, as designed by the Lancaster architects Paley and Austin, but the unique curved-roof waiting shelter on the Down platform was not erected until 1902, following complaints from local residents about the lack of cover. When the request was first received in January 1901 it was turned down on the grounds that the veranda of the station master's house would suffice, but the directors relented a year later and agreed to spend £30 on a shelter. The original station master's house at the north end of the Down platform collapsed into the Esk after the First World War and was replaced by another, now known as *Heron Creek*. The main buildings on the Up platform at Bootle were rebuilt in the only recognisable FR "company style", a Paley and Austin design first used at Greenodd and Haverthwaite and repeated at Sellafield, Drigg and Ravenglass; the Bootle downspout hoppers carry the inscription *18FR73*. The Down platform shelter was similar to that on the Eskmeals Up platform. Silecroft received a new wooden building on the Up platform while the old ramshackle W&FJR buildings on the Down side remained rather longer, until eventually replaced by a larger brick structure.

The station at Millom seems to have been one of the most inadequate on the W&FJR section and in March 1872 the FR directors were reported as "having taken steps" to provide a replacement. Nothing was forthcoming by September that

A mid 1930s view of Eskmeals station looking north towards the Esk viaduct. The typical Furness Paley and Austin-designed building on the Up platform contrasts with the 1902-built shelter which was apparently unique to Eskmeals. The station master's house formerly graced the far end of the Down platform but it was demolished following subsidence.
Photo: CRA Library PA0160

The Furness Railway takes over (1866 - 1923)

The 1969ft bulk of Black Combe looms behind the Station Hotel and 1873 buildings at Bootle. A Furness Railway wooden post signal forms the Down Starter adjacent to the 1874 signal box. FR signals survived at Bootle into the 1970s. In 1904 Bootle Parish Council submitted an application to the FR for a footbridge here for particular use by children on their way to and from school but the issue was deferred. A further request from the Board of Trade followed in 1907, following an accident to a passenger, but the FR was of the view that the ordinary business at Bootle did not justify a footbridge.

Photo: Peter W Robinson Collection

year, when the *Ulverston Mirror* was scathing in its criticism, saying that:

> *It is no uncommon thing for a crowd of passengers to be kept waiting in the wind and rain with no shelter other than a small wooden hut usually odiferous of tarry rope ends, oil cans and tobacco smoke. We would think it a blessing to the community if a squall from the sea or a sudden gust of wind down the Duddon Valley would sweep this execrable erection from its present position.*

Soon after this the W&FJR buildings were replaced with a new construction adjacent to the Up line west of the old station and consisting of two pavilions containing the First Class waiting room and booking office, joined by an open waiting shed. This was quickly found to be inadequate and the next proposal was in the shape of an 1874 design by Paley and Austin; this structure was never built but an almost identical building, still extant, was put up at Askam in 1877. The exact sequence of events with regard to the new buildings is not clear: Stileman reported in February 1875 that additional station accommodation had been completed in the second half of the previous year, presumably referring to the 1872 proposals. Further Paley and Austin plans, dated July 1876, depict an extension to the 1872 building containing a new booking office, waiting room and porters' accommodation, while the original booking office and porters' room were to be rebuilt and incorporated into a new station master's house. The platform elevation of the open waiting

Dating from the 1890s, this view of Millom station shows the 1870s extension to the left of the original Furness building with the open waiting room between the two pavilions. Neither the footbridge nor the Up platform awning has been built, although Down passengers could enjoy the glazed awning shown on the right.
Photo: Stephe Cove Collection

Chapter Six

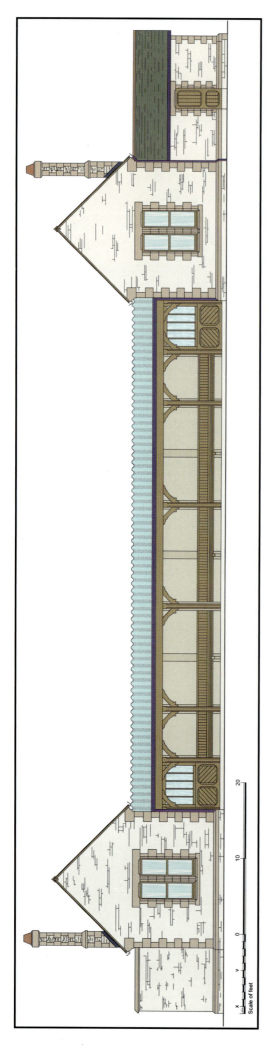

shed was partially boarded in and, at its western end, two further waiting rooms were created for ladies travelling Second Class and gentlemen travelling First. These latter conversions required a wooden lean-to extension on the non-railway side of the building to accommodate water closets. Ladies travelling in superior class were to have had exclusive use of the former First Class waiting room, but the drawing has been altered to show this space used as a parcels office and an office for the station master. The granite buildings would have looked very different from their present appearance when new; over the years weathering has rendered the stone a pale pink colour but when first quarried it would have been quite red.

Despite the development of Newtown, to the south of the railway, the main access to the station remained on the Holborn Hill, or northern, side of the town. There was access to both platforms via steps from the St George's Road bridge which had replaced the level crossing so controversially in 1874 (see Chapter 5). Around the end of the nineteenth century, following great increases in passenger numbers, several changes were made to Millom station, transforming it to a configuration recognisable up until the 1970s. Following numerous complaints from the public about the lack of shelter on the Down platform, the FR agreed to carry out work to remedy this in January 1897. The FR plans showed the construction of a waiting shed incorporating an end screen that reused doors from Ramsden Dock station in Barrow. Perhaps the promotion of Millom Station Master John Jones to Whitehaven, and the appointment of John Morgan from Dalton as his successor in January 1897, prompted the Urban District Council to seek further improvements. In a letter to the FR General Manager the Council asked the railway company to widen the road bridge by 15ft since it was too narrow for the traffic then using it. The FR declined the request but, in the early months of 1901, the Urban District Council sent a deputation to the General Manager, again asking the railway company to widen the road bridge to 40ft. By July it was additionally petitioning the FR for a footbridge between the platforms and a canopy over the Up platform. Throughout the year negotiations took place over sharing the cost of the work, until in February 1902 the FR agreed that, provided the UDC paid for widening the bridge, the railway company would give the necessary land, carry out the widening work, construct a footbridge without cover, remove the steps to the Up platform and modify the steps to the Down platform. The Up platform canopy was deferred. Work commenced on the footbridge in June 1902 and in August that year plans to widen the bridge on the platform side

Paley and Austin - additions & alterations to Millom Station

These are from a series of drawings dated July 1876, showing the extension of the main 1872 buildings to include a new booking office, waiting room, porters' accommodation, toilets and station master's house.

Left - Proposed new station at Millom The replacement for the W&FJR station was planned in 1872 and comprised symmetrical pavilions connected by an open waiting shed, located on the Up platform. This structure still survives within the Millom Discovery Centre.

Page 75
1 - The roadside elevation of the 1876 drawings shows the lean-to extension to accommodate WCs for the two new waiting rooms. The new entrance leads into the waiting room and ticket counter, all of the new building being on made-up ground.

2 - The 1872 booking office and porters' room were extended to provide a house for the station master. Part of the waiting shed has been utilised to form a pantry and scullery and an additional storey has been added.

3 - The Ladies 2nd Class and Gents 1st Class rooms have been created by boarding in part of the old waiting shed. The old western pavilion has been given over to Ladies 1st Class but the plan has been further changed to show its use by the station master and as a parcels office.

Drawn by Alan Johnston, based on drawings in CRA Collection.

The Furness Railway takes over (1866 - 1923)

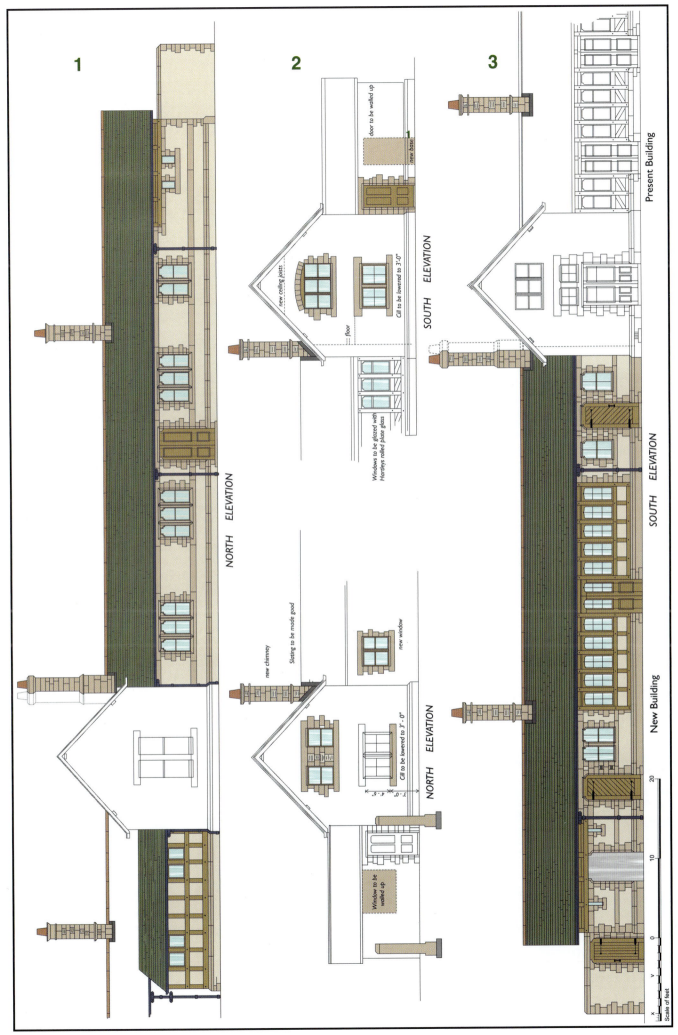

Having opened only two years previously, on 24th August 1904 the Millom station footbridge was struck by an out-of-gauge boiler on its way from the Lonsdale Ironworks at Whitehaven. This photograph shows the hasty repairs needed to prop up the damaged structure. The man on the left of the front group of five is James Holmes, the signalman who was lucky to escape with his life in the 1913 signal box accident.
Photo: Bill Myers Collection

were announced, following a local government inquiry which permitted the UDC to borrow £1,600. Mr WT Lawrence, Clerk to the Council, enthusiastically proclaimed that "the walls of the bridge would be made so as to stop the loafing that now took place on the bridge". A WH Smith bookstall was in place on the station around this time and survived until at least the First World War. The new footbridge was almost demolished on 24th August 1904 when a valve protruding from a large steam boiler being carried on the 11-30am express goods train from Whitehaven to Carnforth caught the decking of the structure. At an FR Traffic & Works Committee meeting on 30th May 1907,

six years after the original MUDC petition for an Up platform canopy, it was noted that in 1906 the station had seen 8,172 more passengers than in 1905 and 24,688 more than in 1896. Accordingly it was agreed to spend some £2,000 on these works. In November 1907 work started on the footbridge cover and a glazed awning on the Up platform. By 1913 the low pressure at the water column on the Up platform was causing delays; consequently a self-contained water tank and column to hold 2,000 gallons was authorised in October that year at an estimated cost of £140. The existing column was recycled for use on the Down line and station yard.

Prominent in this circa 1950 view of Millom's main station buildings is the FR-built glazed awning with hipped roofs in a style reminiscent of the Midland Railway. This was replaced by BR in the 1950s and the low FR platforms rebuilt with concrete edging to modern standards.

Photo: CRA Library Ref SHI042

The Furness Railway takes over (1866 - 1923)

A porter stands beside the curious Up side buildings at Green Road. This wooden structure was unlike any other Furness Railway building and was eventually replaced by the still-extant brick waiting room. The photo was probably taken in the 1930s. The Green Road Station Master, Mr Hewitt, was killed when struck by the loco of a ballast train on 2nd June 1882, whilst attempting to close one of the crossing gates left open by a farmer.
Photo: Stephe Cove Collection

It has not proved possible to tie down all the dates of the improvements to the buildings at Green Road. A note in the Traffic & Works Committee minutes of 7th February 1900 says:

The General Manager referred to the smallness and unsatisfactory condition of the Green Road Booking Office which was quite unfit for the Station Master and Clerk to work in and as it required renewing it was proposed to provide improved accommodation ... at the Engineer's estimated cost of £150 and it was resolved that this work be approved.

The wooden buildings at Green Road, which appear in photographs taken between the Wars, were unlike anything else on the FR system. It is not known when they replaced the original W&FJR buildings, or whether the extant brick buildings were put up in late LMS or early BR days.

Once the W&FJR line had been doubled from Foxfield to Sellafield the FR was able to introduce a much improved timetable. In 1876 Millom (the timetable displayed *Millom [Holborn Hill]* to avoid confusion) saw six weekday trains in each direction, with two Up and three Down trains on Sundays. The service now ran between Whitehaven and Barrow via Furness Abbey and accelerations had taken place: the fastest Millom to Whitehaven train now took 1h 10min, compared with 1h 41min in 1850.

Prior to 1889 many stations and junctions across the country had only very basic signalling arrangements. Following the Armagh railway disaster, in which 78 people were killed and 260 injured, the government intervened in a way previously unheard-of in the history of railways: the Regulation of Railways Act 1889 required all railway companies to install block signalling arrangements and to interlock points and signals. In December 1892 Major-General CS Hutchinson RE, the Board of Trade Inspecting Officer, examined the FR alterations at the end of the two-year period allowed for the work. His report records that at Green Road a new through siding connection had been installed, and a set of level crossing gates provided, worked from a cabin (opened on 30th September 1891) with 16 levers, of which four were spare. The gates, signal box and signals were removed on 31st July 1981, by which time Green Road signal box contained the last surviving Easterbrook frame, although since 13th March 1966 the 'box had served merely as a crossing keeper's cabin/ground frame. Hutchinson noted that at Underhill a crossover road and Down siding connection had been taken out, together with the Down signals, while a new ground frame containing four levers had been provided (opened 4th April 1891 on the Up side six yards from the level crossing). A single siding existed on the Up side until the 1920s; it appears on the 1925 LMS strip map shown in Appendix 1 but is missing from the Ordnance Survey 1:2,500 map of 1924.

At Millom he observed that the siding connections and signals had been remodelled and a new signal box and separate ground frame had been provided. The frame, 220 yards from the signal box, contained four levers and was used to operate the points to the short Up siding, known as the Horse Dock, at the east end of the platform. Opened on 15th June 1891 the new cabin, on the opposite side of the line from its predecessor, contained a 28-lever Railway Signal Company (Fazakerley) frame with five spare levers. The Millom 'box has an intriguing history, being virtually destroyed on 26th February 1913. The weather was foggy and at 7-45 that evening the empty stock from the 6-26pm train from Barrow was being shunted into the carriage shed adjacent to the Up line. At that moment the 4-40pm fast goods from Whitehaven passed the Up home signal, which had been set at danger to protect the shunting move, and ploughed into the rear of the passenger train. The

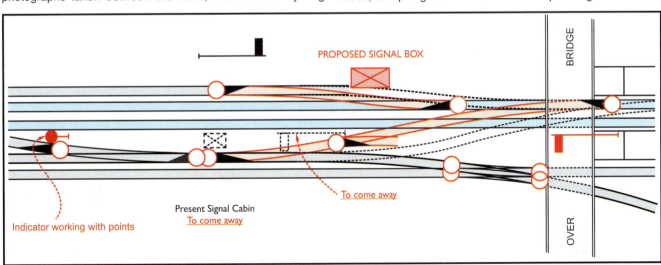

Millom track and signalling alterations 1890 In connection with the opening of the new signal box in June 1891, various track alterations were made to improve access to and from the branch and yard. New work is shown in red; signals and rails to be removed are shown dotted. *Drawn by Alan Johnstone, based on information in the National Archives at Kew.*

77

Chapter Six

Like many similar FR signal boxes, that at Green Road later had the wooden cross-bracing at operating floor level covered with horizontal boards. The LMS introduced name boards on the ends of signal boxes from 1935 and, uniquely on the Furness Section, they were mounted above the eaves. This view was taken on 19th May 1970, by which time the 'box was functioning solely as a crossing keeper's cabin.

Photo: Author

goods engine, 1899-built 0-6-0 No 8, was derailed together with two coaches, one of which struck the signal box and demolished it, leaving just the rear wall and chimney standing. James Holmes, the signalman, was pinned to the chimney by a piece of wood but emerged from the wreckage with only a cut head, the lever frame having protected him from more serious injury. Unsurprisingly, he was severely shocked and was taken to his home at The Hill by horse and trap. The wrecked signal box and overturned coaches completely blocked the line and, shortly after 11-00pm, a breakdown gang arrived with a crane. The locomotive was eventually re-railed and the debris cleared just before noon the following day. After spending some time in a railway convalescent home, Holmes returned to work but avowed that the hastily-built (a brass plaque inside the 'box is dated 25th May 1913) wooden replacement signal box would not

have protected him as well as its stone-built predecessor had done. The original frame was reused and the surviving stone chimney and rear wall retained. Driver Fraser of the goods train was held to be responsible for the accident through not having had his train under sufficient control, given the prevailing weather conditions. The FR Locomotive Superintendent considered that the signal which had been over-run was too close to the fouling point between the main line and the siding. At a later date three extra levers were added to the frame and, by 2002, the building had been fitted with new heaters, double glazing, floor covering

*Right - **Millom second signal box** Dating from 1891, this building replaced the original 'box on the opposite side of the line.*
Drawn by Mike Faulkner, based on a drawing in CRA Collection.

The derailed coach lies on its side against the remains of Millom's second signal box at the end of February 1913. The exposed lever frame and surviving rear wall tower over the gang engaged in clearing up the wreckage. The damage emphasises the lucky escape of signalman James Holmes.
Photo: Hubert Jackson Collection

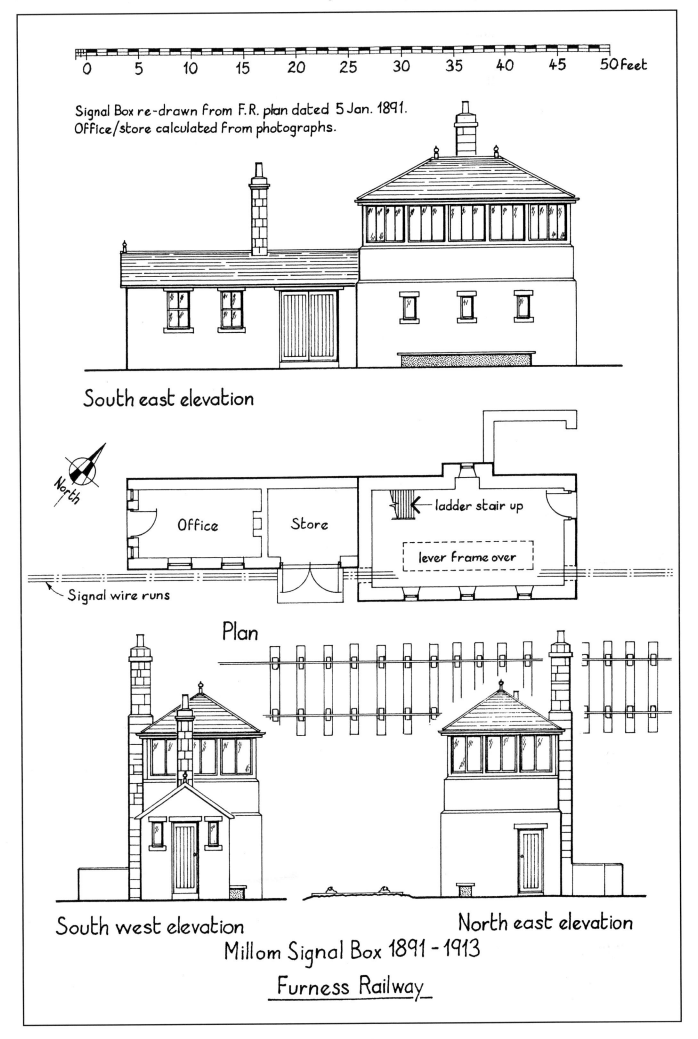

Chapter Six

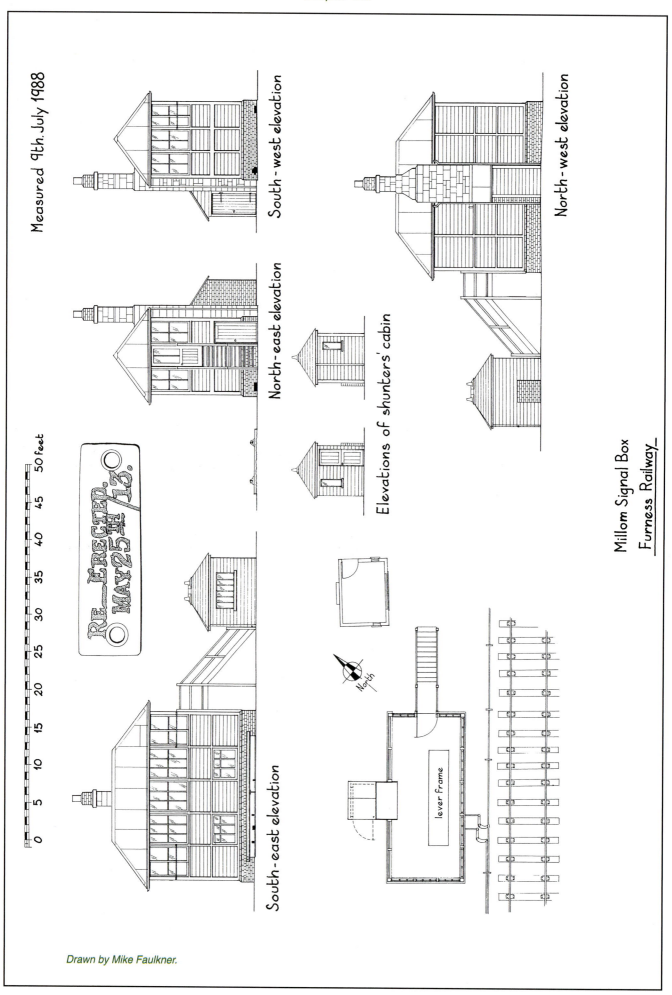

Drawn by Mike Faulkner.

The Furness Railway takes over (1866 - 1923)

Silecroft station looking north from a postcard posted in a 'dreadfully wild and cold' March 1907. The small wooden shelter on the left was eventually replaced by a larger brick-built structure, the Paley and Austin-designed waiting shelter is seen on the Up platform and the signal box dating from August 1882 guards the level crossing. *Author's Collection*

and kitchen area, although the number of levers currently in use is considerably less than in Mr Holmes' day.

The original signal box at Silecroft, which was situated at the end of the Up platform adjacent to the level crossing, was opened on 10th August 1882 with new signalling. It was replaced by the present-day structure, containing a 35-lever Railway Signal Company frame, on the other side of the level crossing on 2nd December 1924. The signal box at Bootle is one of the FR's earliest designs, dating from 1874, and received a new Railway Signal Company frame in 1882. This 12-lever frame was extended to 15 levers before it was replaced with the BR frame from the Nethertown 'box which closed on 25th September 1977.

The penultimate signal box on the line between the Duddon and the Esk is of more than passing interest. *Monk Moors* opened on 2nd December 1897 to control a crossover and the single line to the Eskmeals Gun Range; it had a 10-lever Ransomes & Rapier frame, probably installed second-hand at this site. Known as 'hay rake', 'horse-rake' or 'beer engine' frames, they were uncommon outside the Great Northern and Great Eastern Railways, although the original FR 'box at Sandside on the Arnside - Hincaster Junction line was so equipped. The frame required an extra lever in 1907 when a new siding was laid in for the Eskmeals Granite Company and in October 1932 the 'box was renamed *Vickers Gun Range Sidings*. Reduced to a ground frame on 13th December 1964, the cabin was taken

Vickers Gun Range Sidings signal box opened as Monk Moors in 1897 to serve the connection to the Gun Range and later sidings belonging to the Eskmeals Granite Company. In 1905 it was 'open as required' and in 1915 open four hours a day on weekdays but closed on Sundays. The branch to the Gun Range curves away to the right and is protected by the gate, while Monk Moors Halt can be seen in the distance.

Photo: Geoff Holme Collection

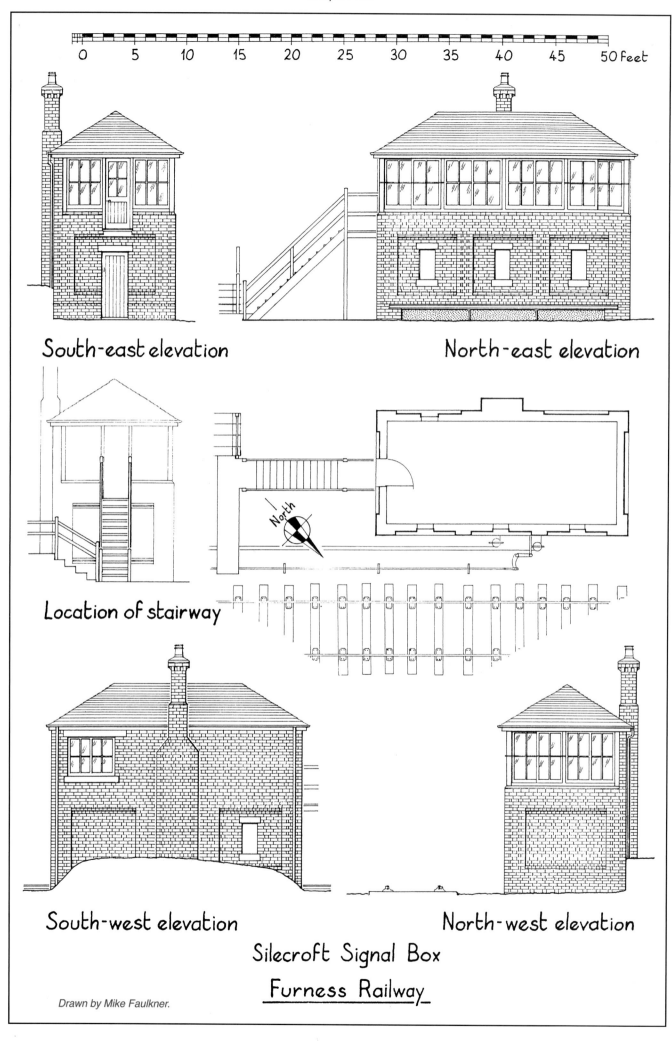

The Furness Railway takes over (1866 - 1923)

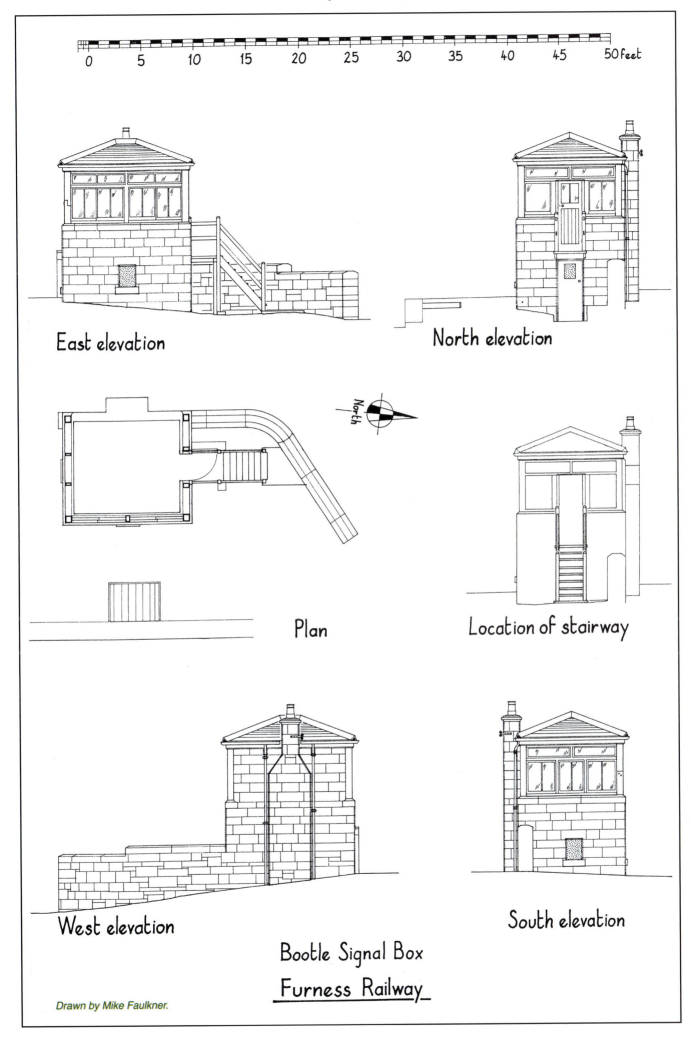

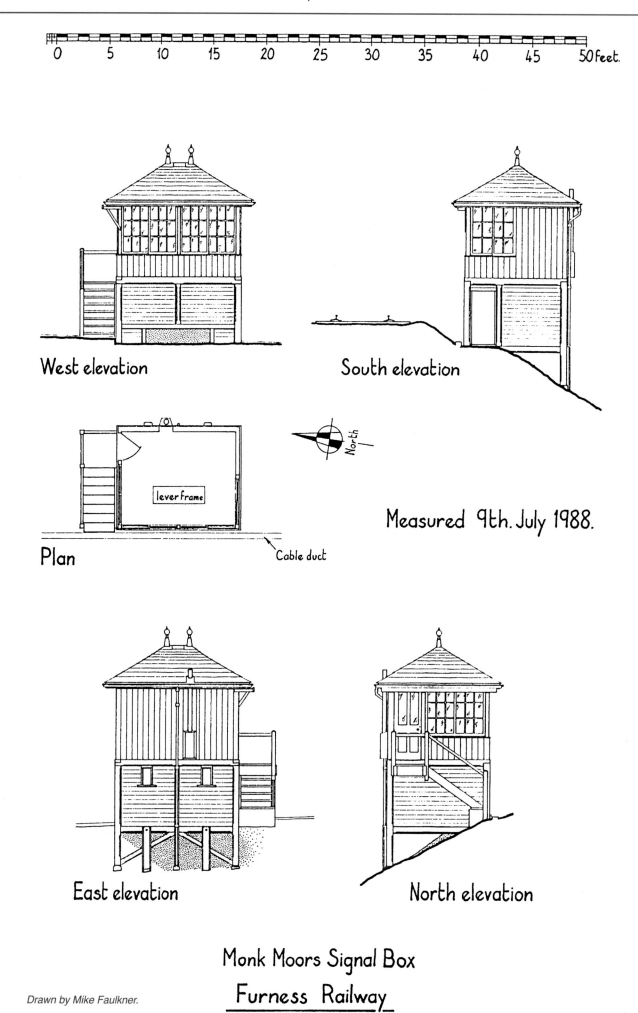

The Furness Railway takes over (1866 - 1923)

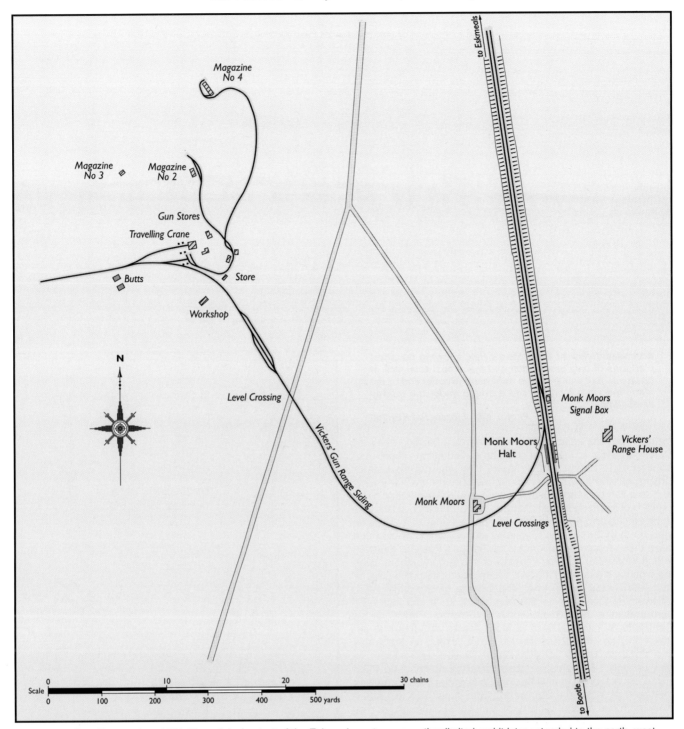

Vickers Gun Range circa 1900 The original extent of the Eskmeals system was rather limited and it later extended to the north, west and south. The proximity of Monk Moors Halt to the Range is clear.

Drawn by Alan Johnstone, based on an Ordnance Survey Map.

out of use following the commissioning of a replacement three-lever ground frame on 24th April 1983. The 'box was removed on 22nd November 1992 and its frame, thought to date from the 1870s, preserved in the National Railway Museum at York. The superstructure was initially privately preserved at Ulverston and then donated to the Furness Railway Trust, before being moved in January 2012 to the Wensleydale Railway to become an operating signal box at Constable Burton.

The signal box at Eskmeals station is something of a conundrum: in the FR Appendix to the Working Time Table (WTT) it appears as a signal box, but not a block post, and is shown in 1905 and 1915 as "closed". By 1931 it was referred to as a "ground frame" and its operating floor was removed on 22nd October that year, leaving the frame exposed on top of the locking room. It was finally abolished on 24th April 1960.

During the 1890s, Vickers, Sons & Maxim of Barrow-in-Furness were searching for a site, close enough to Barrow but sufficiently isolated not to cause safety problems, in order to test-fire medium to large naval guns brought in by rail. In 1897

firing rights were secured from Lowther Estates to permit firing over the foreshore at Eskmeals and the first trials occurred in August that year. Additional land at Monk Moors was purchased from Lowther Estates in the same month and a branch of just over a mile in length to the FR main line was authorised on 1st October 1897. The cost was estimated at £500, to be paid by Vickers, and the line was completed by contractor Coulton W Hunter of Barrow-in-Furness on 23rd March of the following year. Major track construction followed within the site and various locomotives moved on loan from Vickers' main site at Barrow, the connection to the FR being worked by the railway company's locomotives. An "inexpensive" (£60) halt at Monk Moors was constructed for Vickers directors, staff and visitors in 1901, although the normal stopping place for workmen was Eskmeals station, further north. The Halt was closed prior to the First World War, re-opened in 1914 and used regularly until 1919, before closing again until 1940. An undated FR drawing in the Cumbria Archives and Local Studies Centre at Whitehaven shows proposals for the closure of Eskmeals

An undated view of Monk Moors Halt, showing the short platforms of only around 80ft and the almost total lack of facilities. Exit was from the right hand (Bootle) end of the platforms via a footpath and a bridge under the railway embankment.
Photo: CRA Library Ref KER253

station on its site adjacent to the Esk and the building of a new station adjacent to the level crossing at Middleton Place, over a mile nearer Bootle. Monk Moors Halt was not marked for closure but the new station would have been only 800ft away and so it can be safely assumed it too would have closed. The signal box guarding the junction with the Gun Range siding was to be closed and replaced with another serving a tiny Up side yard north of the re-sited Eskmeals station, which would have been much more convenient for the Range. Possibly this was a First World War scheme to deal with the large numbers using the existing station and the halt but, in any case, nothing came of it. Final closure of Monk Moors came on 9th June 1958, followed by Eskmeals on 3rd August 1959. In the last WTT before closure the 5-55am Not Advertised train from Barrow Central to Sellafield arrived at Monk Moors at 6-51am to set down only and the guard was to collect tickets; on Saturdays the 11-50am Bootle to Workington arrived at 11-54am to pick up only. Presumably those travelling southbound used Eskmeals station. Up until the First World War the Range was managed by Vickers at Barrow but, from June 1915 to 1918, it was controlled by the Ministry of Munitions, although Vickers continued to operate it.

Monk Moors signal box served the Gun Range, the Mine Safety Testing Unit, the Scela Gravel Company and the Eskmeals Granite Company, the last having its own siding off the Up line just north of the junction, as detailed below. Between 1912 and 1927 the Mine Safety Unit, served by a northward extension of the Gun Range rail system, conducted research into explosions in mines by constructing large cylinders of one inch boiler plate and igniting coal dust in them: the plant and its 350 yard, 20 inch gauge railway was dismantled at the outbreak of the Second World War. Coulton Hunter, the contractor who built the branch to the main line and who also held a contract for the maintenance of the FR permanent way, had a lease on gravel at the south end of the Gun Range site. The gravel workings were served until about 1928 by a siding extending from the south end of the Gun Range system. The FR is known to have extracted gravel for ballast hereabouts; a note to the Traffic & Works Committee of 1st May 1899 states that the Gun Range siding had been extended and, from 8th April that year, gravel was taken from the foreshore for relaying work at Whitehaven tunnel and Cark. The Broad Oak granite quarry at Waberthwaite had been opened by Ord & Maddison of County Durham in 1876 and this was taken over by the

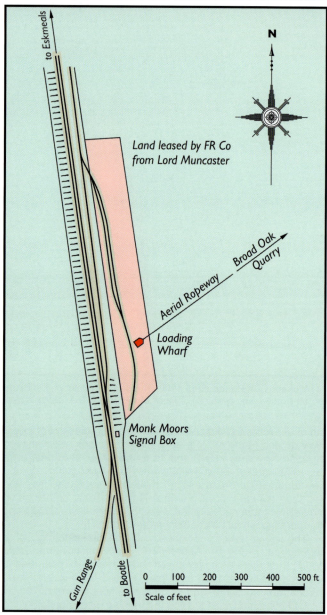

Monk Moors Quarry Siding In 1907 the FR laid these sidings to serve the loading wharf at the end of the Eskmeals Granite Company's aerial ropeway from their Broad Oak Quarry.
Drawn by Alan Johnstone, based on FR map held at Cumbria Archives and Local Studies Centre, Whitehaven.

The Furness Railway takes over (1866 - 1923)

Eskmeals Granite Company in 1905. Previously plans had been produced for a 1½ mile standard gauge tramway linking the quarry to the FR line about 200 yards south of Eskmeals station. The new owners proposed instead to construct a two-mile aerial ropeway from the quarry to about the same place and asked the FR to build an unloading dock with siding accommodation for ten wagons. The Railway's Traffic & Works Committee meeting on 22nd March 1905 noted that the cost of the works would amount to £1,450 and that the Granite Company would not go ahead with the ropeway unless the FR provided accommodation. The FR wanted the traffic but the Granite Company was reluctant to share the costs of the works. After some drawn-out negotiations, in October 1906 the railway company agreed to build a cheaper £500 option with the Granite Company paying £90 per annum rent, on the condition that 10,000 tons or more traffic were generated annually. An FR Signalling Notice, dated 22nd May 1907, indicates that a new siding had been laid in, leading from the Up line just to the north of Monk Moors signal box in order to serve the loading wharf at the end of the ropeway from the quarry. In 1909 the output was described as consisting of granite kerbs, channels, setts, macadam and crushed granite for footpaths, amounting to around 25,000 tons per annum. Amongst quarry machinery were listed 'steam loco cranes' and the aerial ropeway, driven by producer gas. The West of England Cement & Granite Flag Company Ltd established a paving slab works at Monk Moors Siding around 1909 and was supplied with stone from the Eskmeals Granite Company. Business was sufficiently buoyant prior to the First World War for the Granite Company to make representations to the FR for a Millom-Eskmeals workmen's train but the company failed to survive the post-war depression and was in receivership by 24th December 1930. Another concern, the Broad Oak Granite Quarry Company, was registered two years later. It would appear that the new company made little, if any, use of the aerial ropeway or the sidings at Monk Moors, and the connection from the Granite Company's siding to the Up main line was removed on 14th December 1936. The quarry is believed to have closed around 1948.

Expansion of the Eskmeals internal rail system continued between the wars and a variety of steam locomotives was used, drawn from Vickers, Millom Ironworks and, after hostilities had again broken out, from other War Department sites; the first diesel locomotive arrived in 1938. The Ministry of Supply took over the Range during the Second World War with Vickers again running it on an agency basis and in 1951 the government purchased the site. During the War the hostel built for workers at Vickers' ammunition filling factory at Hycemoor was taken over by the Admiralty as *HMS Macaw* and used by the Royal Naval Air Service for holding, retraining and converting aircrew trained in the USA and Canada. After the War most of the steam locomotives were sold on, the last going to Millom Ironworks in 1959. Thereafter diesels were acquired from other government establishments, culminating in the arrival of *Millom Castle* in 1985 and *Muncaster Castle* in 1987. The last regular workings over the branch were in 1989, the last use of the connection to the main line being by the Ministry of Defence crane to assist in heavy repairs to Ravenglass viaduct and station bridge during March and April 1993. Internal rail traffic ceased in 1994 and the branch was lifted during the summer of that year.

The public timetable for 1st July to 30th September 1895 showed five weekday Whitehaven to Carnforth trains stopping at Millom, a further three to Barrow, Dalton or Ulverston and one terminating working from Whitehaven. Three of the Whitehaven trains conveyed through carriages to London Euston, Leeds, Manchester Exchange and Liverpool Lime Street. Seven Down trains terminated at Whitehaven, all but one originating at Carnforth, and there was a single Ulverston train terminating at Millom. There were rather fewer through carriages on to the Furness line than there were off it: Millom passengers could benefit from two trains carrying through carriages from Leeds to Whitehaven and three through workings from London Euston, Manchester Exchange and Wigan. The number of trains remaining at Millom at the end of the day resulted in the FR Locomotive Superintendent requesting a carriage shed. In May 1906 the company agreed to construct a shed 420ft long and 15ft wide at an estimated cost of £900 (although Messrs Main's accepted tender was for £600) adjacent to the Up line

Hudswell Clarke 1742 of 1946 is seen outside Millom goods shed in 1969. This locomotive had worked at Eskmeals Gun Range, Hodbarrow and the ironworks before being saved for preservation at an ultimately abortive scheme for a steam centre in the goods yard. In 2012 No 1742 was in working order at the Buckinghamshire Railway Museum.

Photo: Hubert Jackson Collection

Chapter Six

On 4th September 1953 the former FR No 1, now BR 52494 and still carrying a Furness boiler with round-top firebox, sits on Millom's 60ft turntable. Built by North British in 1913, 52494 had less than three years to go before withdrawal. The loco carries Target 99, Moor Row's lunchtime trip to Millom which shunted the sidings en route.
Photo: VR Webster/Kidderminster Railway Museum

on the Silecroft side of the signal box. This was the shed into which empty stock was being propelled when it was struck by the goods train in the signal box accident of 1913. By April 1910 a Millom inhabitant could look forward to six weekday passenger trains between Whitehaven and Carnforth and a further three Millom to Carnforth services. In the opposite direction the same number of trains departed for Whitehaven, two services from Carnforth terminated at Millom and there was an unbalanced arrival from Coniston. Should the Edwardian traveller have wished to venture beyond Furness, three of the Whitehaven services carried through carriages to and from London Euston and St Pancras. For those in need of transport to more mundane destinations, Millom UDC petitioned the FR, in October 1911, to extend the 5-13am Kirkby to Barrow Workmen's train to start from Millom and for the men to enjoy cheap fares. The railway company was concerned that to do so would involve seven light and seven loaded train miles each weekday at a cost of £7 per week but was prepared to do as requested, provided the Council gave a guarantee of not less than 36 weekly tickets sold at four shillings (20p) each. The trains started in the following month but were withdrawn in 1912 because of lack of patronage. In May 1914 the Property Owners Association of Millom met the FR's General Manager, Alfred Aslett, to seek the reintroduction of cheap workmen's fares. Aslett offered a better deal than previously, quoting a minimum fare of 3s 6d (17½p), provided the Association could guarantee 15 weekly ticket sales on a train departing at 5-10am. Millom was reported as having 200 empty houses at the time, while Barrow had none and was suffering from overcrowding. Within two months, the advent of hostilities would overtake the problem of empty houses.

Turning to freight patterns at the end of the nineteenth century, the FR WTT from 1st July to 30th September 1891 shows an amazing twelve Up goods workings serving Millom on weekdays. Of these, seven originated in the town, three terminated and two passed *en route*. In the Down direction seven goods trains ended their journeys at Millom, three started there and two called on their way to Preston Street goods depot in Whitehaven. As can be seen, the majority of the traffic was to and from points south of the town. Reflecting the prosperity of the two iron companies, the Hodbarrow branch was served by seven weekday trains in each direction.

In view of the large number of trains, both passenger and goods, starting from and terminating at Millom, the FR installed a 42ft turntable in the early 1890s to the west of the road bridge. By 1900 this needed to be lengthened to 46ft to accommodate larger locomotives and, on 18th August 1923 the LMS installed a 60ft turntable, originally destined for Corkickle, on a slightly different site. In February 1900 the Superintendent of the Line complained that the limited siding accommodation at Millom was causing delays to traffic; general traffic had increased by 9,042 tons in the previous four years and in the same period Millom Ironworks traffic had increased by 137,485 tons. The FR agreed to spend £540 on additional sidings. Two years later the General Manager was asked to provide an engine shed at Millom to save light engine working to and from Barrow, but it was felt that the small number of engines involved did not justify the cost. Despite a fall in iron production immediately following the turn of the century, and the consequent reduction in mineral traffic, general traffic continued to rise at Millom during the early years of the twentieth century. In July 1903 a deputation of the town's tradesmen to the FR reported that cartage work was being compromised by goods carts having to deliver parcels received by passenger trains. The goods tonnage delivered during the first half of 1901 had amounted to 1,892 tons and this had risen to 2,095 tons in the same period in 1903, while 20,312 parcels had been delivered in 1902. Consequently a parcels delivery van was allocated to the town in October 1903, the horses for the carts and van being housed in the stables immediately adjacent to the Lancashire Road wall of the goods yard at the end of Lapstone Road. In 1897 the FR Engineer's Office had prepared plans for an extension to the goods shed to cater for the increased general merchandise handled but this was never built. The original building was found sufficient until its closure in 1970.

The advent of the First World War in 1914 was to put unimagined pressures on the Furness Railway serving, as it did, the Vickers shipbuilding and engineering works, the docks at Barrow, numerous ironworks and iron ore mines working at virtually full capacity and the Gun Range at Eskmeals. In 1915 Vickers despatched and received more than double the traffic it had handled in 1913 and by 1916 it was up again by more than 50%; while much of this went south from Barrow, the traffic between Barrow and Eskmeals would have shown a significant

The Furness Railway takes over (1866 - 1923)

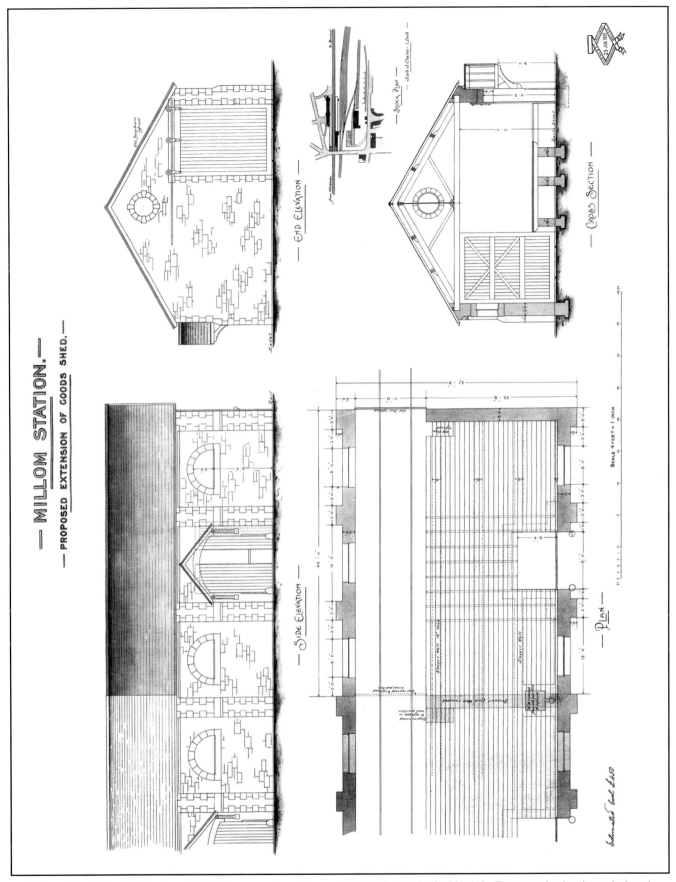

Millom Goods Shed Extension This 1897 proposal would have extended the goods shed by 45ft. The extension has been designed to harmonise with the original building but was never constructed. The goods shed accommodated two cranes, each of 30cwt capacity.
Drawn by Alan Johnston, based on a drawing in CRA Collection.

The last vestiges of FR motive power. Around 1950, 0-6-0 52510 starts its journey from Millom back to its West Cumberland home and is about to cross over on to the Down line with a Class J through mineral or empty wagon train. A 4F 0-6-0 with sliding top cover on its tender sits in the Up siding.

Photo: CRA Library Ref SHI193

increase. In order to provide the additional workforce at Vickers trains used by around 2,000 workmen were run from Dalton, Ulverston, Lindal, Askam, Kirkby and Millom to Barrow Island Road station (often referred to as *Shipyard station*). Driven from their own country by the conflict, many Belgians moved into Millom and the Furness district from 1914 onwards. Vickers at one time employed around 900 of them which necessitated extra trains from Grange, Kent's Bank and Cark. As recalled in Chapter 4, Spanish haematite was imported through Barrow and by 1917 between six and ten trains a day were being carried round the coast to the ironworks in West Cumberland. Perversely, these trains would have crossed similar trains of iron ore travelling south from the mines of West Cumberland to the furnaces at Millom. The Millom & Askam Hematite Iron Company traffic rose from 376,403 tons in 1913 to 386,147 tons in 1915 and then to 498,781 tons in 1916, the latter representing a 33% increase over the pre-war figure. In October 1915 the General Manager reported to the Traffic and Works Committee that so much additional traffic from the LNWR/FR Joint Line (the former Whitehaven, Cleator & Egremont Railway) was being handled at Millom that an additional siding was necessary. He noted that, in the period from January to October 1915, 17,509 wagons had been forwarded from the West Cumberland district to stations south of Carnforth compared with 8,804 in the same period in 1914; this represented a massive 99% increase.

As the War dragged on, the 1917 Government Coal Transport Reorganisation Scheme divided the country into 20 zones in order to reduce coal traffic mileage. Unfortunately the existing signalling arrangements limited the number of extra trains from Cumberland, Durham and Northumberland that could traverse the erstwhile W&FJR line *en route* to the Furness area. In 1917 the FR Board agreed (at an estimated cost of £350) to the construction of a new signal box at Stangrah (named after a nearby farm), 2 miles 783 yards from Silecroft, to break up the long (5 miles 539 yards) block section between Silecroft and Bootle. The eight lever (including three spares) Stangrah 'box opened, on the Up side, rather late in the War on 22nd July 1918 and had a very short existence, closing on 30th June in the following year. It was not demolished for several years and its base was later used as a platelayers' hut. As part of the 1917 scheme, a Down loop opened north of Bootle signal box on the same day that the Stangrah 'box opened.

The War also put pressure on the separate railway companies to collaborate in order to make savings on the use of men and locomotives. An observer at Millom during those difficult years might have noted Maryport & Carlisle locomotives working the Up Mail train from Whitehaven to Carnforth as far as Millom, where it arrived at 7-57pm. He might also have noted London & North Western engines due to arrive from Tebay at 8-05am and 4-10pm with coke traffic for the ironworks. In 1917 several interesting goods workings were reported: the FR worked four return trips a day between Barrow and Carlisle (and two more if required), the M&CR ran one train each way between Carlisle and Barrow and the North Eastern two Carlisle-Millom returns. In 1918 LNWR motive power would have been seen passing through Millom on six Down and five Up Workington freight workings, while LNWR locos were in charge of two Millom-Lindal trains in each direction. There was a single M&CR working in each direction. For the duration of the hostilities the Admiralty commissioned special trains to carry coal from South Wales to Grangemouth in Scotland, there to be transhipped to Scapa Flow for the Grand Fleet. Colloquially known as *Jellicoe Specials*, most of these trains and the returning empty wagons were routed over Shap, but it is known that empties at least were routed via the Cumberland coast to save paths on the main line. In a reflection of the need for Cumberland ore and pig iron, signal boxes were kept open longer and there were four LNWR workings each way on Sundays and ten weekday trains each way on the Hodbarrow branch.

An accident at Millom just after the Armistice gives an insight into train working at that time. At about 6-20pm on 20th November 1918 the 5-30pm Up mixed train from Ravenglass, hauled by 1907-built FR six-coupled goods engine No 5, divided as it was entering the station and the rear portion overran the front, injuring a passenger. The passenger portion of the train, comprising a six-wheel passenger van and three six-wheel coaches, was followed by 25 goods wagons and a brake van, in which the guard was travelling. The Board of Trade Inspector deduced that the action of the guard in screwing down the brake had resulted in a coupling shearing between the passenger van and the coaches and that there should have been three more similar brake vans spaced at intervals between the goods vehicles. He noted that the failure of the FR to comply with the regulations had no bearing on the accident as experience gained during the war suggested that the requirement on the number of brake vans could be relaxed.

The cessation of hostilities did not herald prosperity for the FR; between 1920 and 1921 the volume of iron and steel castings carried fell from nine million tons to three and a half million tons, passenger traffic was down by about 30% and goods and mineral traffic fell by more than 50%. By the time wartime government

The Furness Railway takes over (1866 - 1923)

In the 1940s Furness 0-6-0 12510, with Lancashire and Yorkshire Railway Belpaire boiler, brings a train out of Silecroft goods yard on to the Down line. This was the last FR loco to remain in service, being withdrawn in August 1957. The 1924 signal box guards the level crossing and pointwork and the towering mass of Black Combe forms a majestic background.
Photo: CRA Library Ref SHI190

control ended on 15th August 1921 the FR, in common with most of the country's railway companies, was still in a run-down condition after more than four years of war. Four days later the Railways Act 1921 received the Royal Assent, spelling out the imminent demise of the FR and its absorption into one of the 'Big Four' grouped companies. Immediately before the Grouping of 1st January 1923 the last FR Working Timetable (published on 2nd October 1922) shows twelve Up passenger trains, and 15 in the Down direction, calling at Millom on Mondays to Fridays. The service was essentially between Carnforth and Whitehaven Bransty with around five trains between Millom and Barrow only. The first Up train was the 6-15am to Barrow Shipyard, made up of twelve six-wheel 50-seat coaches which returned to Millom at 6-05pm (1-15pm on Saturdays). RR Mester, writing in *Railway World* in April 1982, recalls that "there was a special aura attached to the Barrow Island workmen's trains . . . redolent of twist pipe tobacco and . . . Woodbine cigarettes, characteristics of this stock were hard wooden seating and straight backs extending to shoulder level". The first Down train was the 4-40am from Carnforth, *The Whitehaven Sorting Tender* (usually referred to as *The Mail*), arriving at Millom at 6-13am.

The October 1922 WTT shows 14 goods trains in the Up direction consisting of four fast goods stopping for water and the others starting from, or terminating at, Millom - five Millom to Barrow, Ulverston, Plumpton Junction or Carnforth workings and five arrivals from Whitehaven, the West Cumberland Joint Lines and Monk Moors. Similarly, there were 14 northbound goods trains: three fast goods stopping for water only, seven departures for the Joint Lines, Whitehaven and the solitary Monk Moors turn and four arrivals from Lindal Ore Sidings or Barrow Yard. It can be seen that most of the traffic was either destined for the town (iron ore, coke, limestone, coal and general goods) or originated there (iron ore, pig iron and returning empties). Ore traffic from West Cumberland was more significant than it had been in the previous century, being handled by four Fast Goods trains from Sellafield, two being Barrow turns, one covered by Workington and one by Moor Row. Loaded wagons from Ullcoats were tripped to Egremont to be made into train loads, before returning south to the junction with the FR line at Sellafield, while the layout at Florence Pit Sidings did not require the short northbound journey. In 1922 there were six trips from the station to the Hodbarrow Mineral Sidings on the Mains using two different locos (FR 0-6-0s at this time) off Barrow to Millom goods turns, the first leaving Millom at 10-05am and the last returning there at 6-00pm.

The year 1922 was to be the last for the Furness Railway and it is therefore appropriate to recall a piece in the *Millom Gazette* of 16th January that year. The editor, seemingly convinced that the LNWR was about to take over the FR, regarded this as an opportune moment to once more dust down the idea of crossing Morecambe Bay and the Duddon estuary. His assumption that Millom needed help was undoubtedly true but his notion of the LNWR's rebuilding of the Furness line as part of a through route to Scotland via the Solway viaduct was around 100 years late and somewhat fanciful. By the end of the year the FR was no more, and the next chapter covers Millom's place in the history of the Furness and West Cumberland Section of the London, Midland & Scottish Railway.

91

Chapter Seven

On 2nd April 1966 the SLS/MLS Lakes and Fells Railtour is held momentarily at Millom as ex-works 9F 92233 heads north with Covhops for Whitehaven Corkickle. The railtour had experienced atrocious weather on the journey from Manchester over the Settle & Carlisle to Penrith and then to Workington via Keswick so that it was some two hours late at Millom. Upperby-based Ivatt 2MTs 46458 and 46426 hauled the train from Penrith via Keswick and the Cumbrian Coast to Arnside, from where 4472 *Flying Scotsman* returned the hapless passengers to Manchester.
Photo: David C Williams

Aspinall LYR 0-6-0 No 52418 of Moor Row shed disturbs the tranquillity of Silecroft station as it heads south with a Class J goods on 1st September 1953. The characteristic Paley and Austin waiting shelter and the FR squirrel seat complete the composition.
Photo: VR Webster/Kidderminster Railway Museum

The Railway after 1923

LMS Furness & West Cumberland Section; war again; British Railways; sixties rationalisation; a twenty-first century railway; the Duddon crossing – a dream still unfulfilled.

> *"...the passenger service is, and has been, for many years losing money in spite of various steps which have been taken to put it on a remunerative basis."*
> J Pollard, BR Divisional Manager 'New Booking Arrangements Barrow-Whitehaven-Carlisle Line', 4th September 1967

ON 1st JANUARY 1923 the Furness Railway, along with 34 other companies, some larger and some smaller, became part of the London Midland & Scottish Railway. The FR found itself in Western B Division along with the Lancashire & Yorkshire (LYR) and Maryport & Carlisle (M&CR) Railways. Initially very little changed, other than the colour of the locomotives and rolling stock and, up until 1930, most of the passenger turns serving Millom continued to be hauled by FR 4-4-0s, 0-6-0s and the various tank engines, the indigenous 0-6-0s maintaining the much-reduced goods traffic of the post-war period. The FR passenger locomotives were scrapped fairly rapidly, to be replaced by LNWR and Midland designs, themselves displaced from their normal haunts by more modern machines. By the mid-1930s these too had gone and most of the local passenger turns were in the hands of LMS 2-6-4Ts. The FR goods types were longer-lasting than the passenger engines but many of the older 0-6-0s were scrapped, to be replaced by LYR, LNWR and Midland Railway motive power of the same wheel arrangement.

The LMS modified the Furness Section passenger train pattern to include several through trains beyond Whitehaven to and from Workington and Carlisle; the timetable from 17th July to 10th September 1933 showed 15 Up trains and 16 Down calling at Millom on weekdays. The number of Millom-Barrow services had reduced slightly compared with the last FR timetable of 1922. Millom inhabitants could still enjoy a number of through carriages off the Furness Section to and from destinations such as London, Leeds, Liverpool, Manchester and Bradford, although some of these were only available during the summer months. In the last LMS timetable immediately prior to the Second World War (3rd July to 24th September 1939) the number of Up trains had increased to 17, with 18 in the Down direction. In the Up direction there were through carriages to Manchester, London and Morecambe, with through Down services from Manchester, Leeds, Liverpool and London (plus Morecambe on Saturdays). By the 1930s most of the FR non-corridor coaches used between Carnforth and Whitehaven had been replaced by old, but more comfortable, corridor vehicles of LNWR and Midland Railway origins. The last LMS timetable before nationalisation was issued on 6th October 1947 and showed a reduction to eleven weekday trains in the Up direction with twelve in the Down for Millom passengers. The service was mainly between Barrow and Workington with three Up and two Down Millom-Barrow journeys, reflecting the needs of workmen and shoppers. Through carriages still served Euston, Manchester and Liverpool.

Turning to goods traffic, the *LMS (Western Division) Working Timetable [WTT] 9th July to 30th September 1923* is, unsurprisingly, little different from the final FR version. In the Up direction there were 17 goods workings, with all but three of them originating or terminating at Millom. The seven arrivals were from Eskmeals, Whitehaven, Workington and the Joint Lines (Egremont, Moor Row, Sellafield and Gillfoot). Those originating at Millom were destined for Barrow (three), Carnforth (two), Lindal Ore Sidings and Plumpton Junction. There was the same number of trains in the northbound direction and, again, all but three originated or terminated at Millom. The eight arrivals started at Barrow Yard (three), Lindal Ore Sidings (three), Park Sidings and Carnforth, while the six departures were for Eskmeals, Whitehaven, the Joint Lines (three) and Workington. Extra trains were run on Thursdays for cattle traffic to Ulverston and Whitehaven. The significance of the ironworks traffic is plain to see.

By 1936 *the LMS (Western Division) WTT 4th May to 27th September* showed a reduction to 13 Up freight workings, all but five of which terminated or originated at Millom. Three trains, Targets 92 and 104 from Moor Row and Target 101 from Sellafield, dealt with the Joint Lines traffic to Millom and Target 93 was a stopping freight from Whitehaven; two workings to Barrow and one each to Lindal Sidings and Carnforth started their journeys at the town. In the Down direction eleven freights served Millom, three of which called *en-route*. The four trips worked back to West Cumberland, together with an additional through freight to Workington, whilst there were two arrivals from Barrow and one from Plumpton Junction. Each district had its own *Trip Book* which detailed shunting engine and local trip workings; locomotives engaged in these duties were required to carry a *target* (board) corresponding to the number shown in the book. Signalmen would report arrivals and departures to Control using the target number carried on the front of the locomotive.

Apart from iron ore, the other inward traffic to the ironworks was coke (mainly from County Durham) and limestone from Redhills and Goldmire quarries. Coke from the North East was hauled from Tebay, via Hincaster Junction and Arnside to Lindal Ore Sidings, from where there were up to four daily trip workings to Millom with a corresponding number of returning empties. Limestone from Redhills was carried over the company's internal railway and that from Goldmire came via trip workings from Park sidings, near Askam.

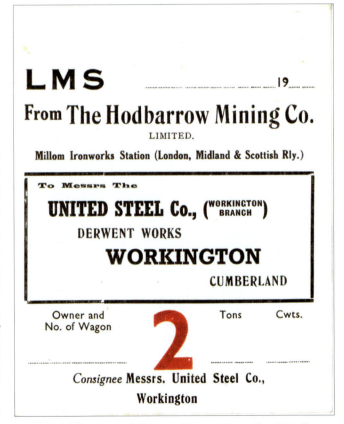

This LMS wagon label would have been fixed to the underframe of a loaded wagon of haematite from Millom to Workington. The LMS loco would have collected its load from the Hodbarrow sidings but notice that its point of origin is described as Millom Ironworks Station.
Peter Holmes Collection

93

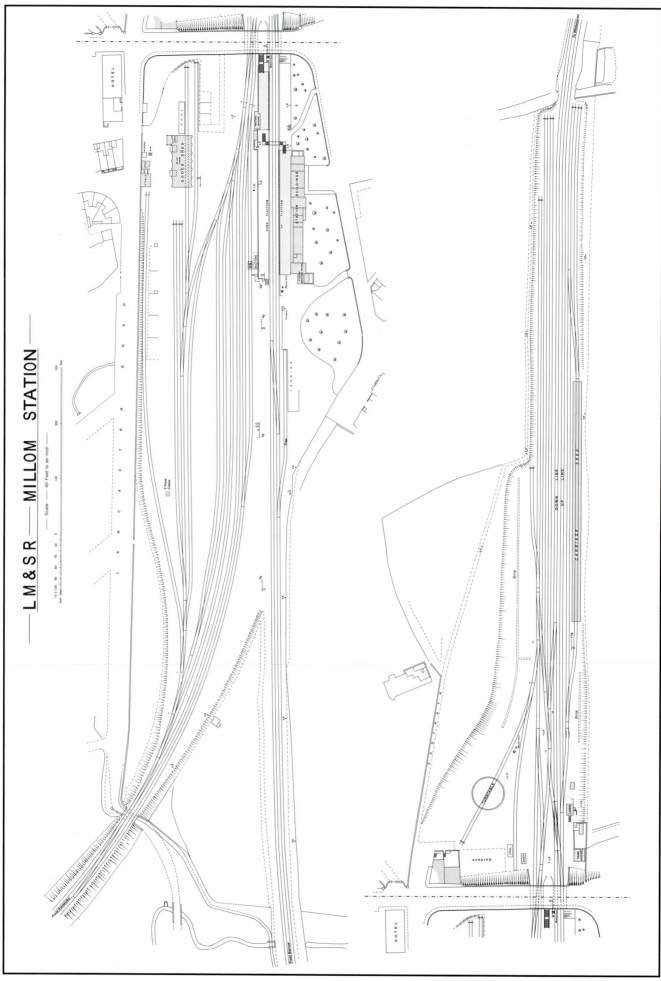

LMS Plan of Millom Station and sidings

Redrawn by Alan Johnstone.

The Railway after 1923

The Aspinall L&YR 0-6-0s were allocated to Workington and Moor Row sheds from the mid-1930s. 52201 in early BR livery shunts Millom yard on 24th August 1953. No 2 Home signal on the right was on the Hodbarrow branch and was fitted with a telephone in connection with working the branch.

Photo: VR Webster/ Kidderminster Railway Museum

For most of the late FR, LMS and early BR periods the Hodbarrow branch was worked as part of a weekdays-only Barrow Target and involved five or six return trips between Millom station yard and Hodbarrow sidings (ten minutes) or the ironworks (five minutes). The LMS 1928 arrangements involved Target 17, the Millom shunting engine (FR, LNWR or LYR 0-6-0), leaving the yard on its first trip to Hodbarrow at 9-50am, working four more return trips and finally returning to Millom at 5-20pm.

The LMS Sectional Appendix to the WTT Western Division, March 1937 gives the following instructions for working the branch:

The Mineral Agent's office is open from 8-15am to 5-30pm (SX), 1-20pm (SO). (Closed on Sundays).

Telephones are fixed on each side of the outer home signal posts for the purpose of communicating with the Mineral Agent's office and Millom Station signal box. When the Mineral Agent's office is open, drivers must not pass the outer home signals until permission has been obtained by the guard, shunter or person in charge from this office or from the signalman at Millom Station signal box, and the signal has been taken off. In the case of telephone failure or other circumstances preventing the signals being taken off, no train must pass these signals at danger until verbal permission has been obtained.

When the Mineral Agent's office is closed, the driver must obtain the train staff from the signalman at Millom Station signal box, and this will be his authority to pass signals at danger except the branch up home signal.

The guard or shunter is responsible for returning the staff to the Millom Station signalman when the work on the branch is completed.

The branch was worked by "one engine in steam or two or more engines coupled together" and the staff referred to was round and coloured red.

Following the same pattern as during the First World War, the advent of hostilities in 1939 found Millom and the remaining ironworks in Furness and West Cumberland working at full capacity. Traffic between Vickers at Barrow and Eskmeals again rose and large quantities of ammunition were carried. During the closing months of the War an incident occurred about a quarter of a mile south of Bootle station which could have obliterated the station and resulted in a greater loss of life than it did. Shortly after 10-00pm on the evening of 22nd March 1945 a through freight train from Workington to Liverpool Bankfield was passing through the station when the fireman, Norman Stubbs, noticed one of the wagons fiercely ablaze. The first seven of the 58 wagons contained depth charges being delivered from the Admiralty's Camerton Sidings (on the former Cleator & Workington Junction Railway) and it was one of these, marshalled sixth from the engine, which was alight. The guard and driver brought the train to a stop: Stubbs ran back and uncoupled behind the burning wagon, before returning to the footplate as the locomotive drew the first six clear of the rest of the train. About 80 yards on, they stopped again and Stubbs managed to uncouple the offending vehicle where, in his own words, "the heat was terrific, flames were coming out of the bottom and sides". Again they moved about 80 yards forward with the remaining five wagons in order to distance themselves from the blaze and Stubbs then went forward on foot to place detonators on the Down line to stop any northbound trains. He had not gone very far when the wagon exploded, throwing him through the air and on to the side of the track "and a huge wall of debris was blotting out the moon". Shaken, but not seriously injured, he managed to get up and continued placing his detonators. Returning to the scene, Stubbs found a crater 105 feet long, between 45 feet and 60 feet wide and about 50 feet deep and 60 yards of double track torn up. Unfortunately his

The scene just south of Bootle station after a wagon loaded with nine tons of high explosive had detonated in March 1945. The wagons detached by Norman Stubbs and Harold Goodall stand at the edge of the 50ft deep crater caused by the explosion. Amazingly, the hole was filled in and single line working implemented less than two days after the explosion and within 68 hours normal operation had been resumed.   *Photo: CRA Library Ref M10412*

Chapter Seven

driver Harold Goodall had been killed by the blast. Not knowing that Southward, the Bootle signalman, had already sent the code 'Stop and Examine' and telephoned Silecroft 'box, Stubbs then boarded the damaged locomotive, Midland Railway 3F No 3579, and headed south with the intention of stopping the northbound train in section by putting down more detonators. One can only imagine his relief on arriving at Silecroft to see the passenger train standing in the station. But for Goodall's and Stubbs' timely and selfless actions, all seven wagons could well have exploded and for his heroism Stubbs was awarded the George Medal by the King later that year. The crater was filled in and a single line was opened for traffic by 7-00pm on 24th March; this involved shifting between 2,000 and 3,000 cubic yards of material. Within the remarkably short period of 68 hours normal working was resumed, albeit under speed restriction. 52 depth charges, comprising 9¼ tons of high explosive, had detonated causing extensive, though superficial, damage to HMS *Macaw*, the Admiralty shore establishment 300-400 yards away. A large amount of glass was broken in Bootle Station as well as in the villages of Bootle (1,500 yards distant) and Hycemoor (1,100 yards distant). The official report concluded that the cause of the fire was a spark from the engine lodging in, and igniting, the wagon sheet. As a consequence of this incident, and a similar one near Selby a month later, enginemen were to be informed when explosives were being conveyed, the 'Explosives' labels were to return to the distinctive peace-time style and consideration was to be given to re-introducing the restriction, relaxed during war-time, of marshalling explosive loads in the middle of the train.

The Transport Act 1947 could be seen as completing the programme started by the 1923 Grouping and on 1st January 1948 British Railways came into being as part of the Labour government's policy to nationalise public services. By the time that BR was operating Furness line services through Millom, virtually all local passenger trains were in the hands of the Fowler, Stanier and Fairburn varieties of 2-6-4T, Stanier Class 5MTs had become more prevalent, Ivatt Class 4MT 2-6-0s from Workington were seen and some of the more prestigious trains carrying through carriages were graced by *Patriot*, *Jubilee* and *Royal Scot* 4-6-0s.

During the early 1950s BR raised the old FR platforms at Millom station, installed concrete platform walling, repaired the rotten Down platform awning and replaced the elegant hipped-roof glazed awning over the Up platform with a more utilitarian offering but, at the same time, retained the original supports which still carry the FR monogram in their spandrels. The awning and passenger facilities on the Down platform were demolished around 1970 and in 1971 the awning was re-erected at Ravenglass on the Ravenglass & Eskdale Railway. There it continues to do the job for which it was intended when built in the nineteenth century.

There were only minor changes to the passenger service during the 1950s. The BR timetable for 17th June to 8th September 1963 (the last to be exclusively covered by steam) showed eleven Up trains and nine Down on weekdays, the pattern little changed from the final LMS timetable of 16 years before. The 6-20am still carried workmen in their "reserved" seats (woe betide those who sat in someone else's place!) to Island Road station in Barrow, the first Down train was *The Mail* (or, in official parlance, the *Preston-Whitehaven Travelling Post Office*) at 6-06am and most services ran between Carnforth and Workington. There were the same Millom-Barrow workings as well as through carriages to Birmingham, Euston, St Pancras, Lancaster, Manchester and Liverpool. In the Down direction there were through carriages from Euston, Lancaster, Manchester, Morecambe, Crewe and Liverpool; as in earlier years, some of the through services were for the summer season only.

Prior to the opening of Wyndham School at Egremont in 1964 most young people in the huge Millom Rural District received their secondary education at Millom School and BR laid on a non-advertised train for their use. The 14th June 1965 -17th April 1966 Working Timetable shows an 08-00 departure

Millom Signalling Diagram *This diagram is marked 29th June 1945 but the signals suggest it dates from around 1960. Original in Geoff Holme collection, redrawn by Alan Johnstone.*

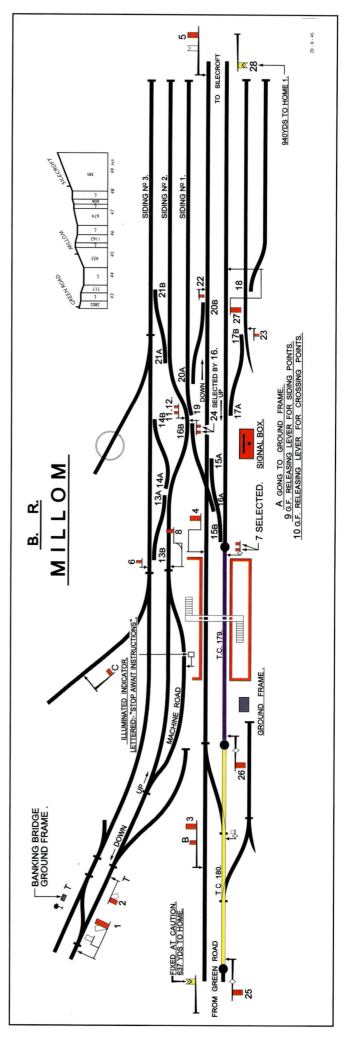

The Railway after 1923

On 19th July 1961 Fairburn 2-6-4T 42179 emerges from beneath the cast iron girders of the St George's Road bridge on the 3-28pm Barrow to Sellafield, due to depart Millom at 4-10pm. The second opening in the bridge on the right gave access to the Hodbarrow branch and the goods yard. 42179 was to survive at Barrow for another four years.
Photo: CRA Library Ref PES364

from Seascale, calling at all stations and arriving at Millom at 08-34. The stock remained in the sidings before heading north at 16-10 for Workington, where it arrived at 17-47, but on Fridays the departure was three minutes later and the train only went as far as Seascale. The goings-on in the non-corridor stock enjoyed a certain notoriety!

Modernisation of a sort came to the area in early 1962 when the first Metropolitan Vickers Co-Bo (later Class 28) diesels arrived at Barrow, having been displaced from more prestigious duties elsewhere. By September 1963 they were all nominally allocated to Barrow shed, although some were out-stationed at Workington. The diesels worked to the old steam schedules on passenger and goods trains, but were notorious for their unreliability and ability to set the Barrow shed roof on fire! During 1966-67 they were transferred to Carlisle but continued on the Cumbrian Coast routes until, by September 1968, they had all been withdrawn, many before the steam locomotives they were designed to replace. One locomotive, D5705, survives in preservation at the East Lancashire Railway.

Published on 27th March 1963, *The Reshaping of British Railways*, the infamous *Beeching Report*, saw no future for the passenger service between Barrow and Whitehaven due to the losses incurred, although freight traffic was to be retained. The whole of the Cumbrian Coast line from Carnforth to Carlisle was shown as carrying between 5,000

On 6th May 1963 Metrovick Co-Bo D5715 works 1L12, the 9-50am Manchester Victoria to Workington Main (due 3-35pm), at Green Road, where it was scheduled at 1-52pm. The replacement buildings are prominent on the Up platform and the summit of Coniston Old Man can be seen in the far distance. The 20 locos of what became Class 28 were built as part of BR's Pilot Plan during 1958/9 but all had been withdrawn from service ten years later.

Photo: Ron Herbert

97

Chapter Seven

The saviour of the Cumbrian Coast line? A Regional Railways-liveried Class 31 rounds the curve after passing under Moor Bridge at the head of a Barrow Ramsden Dock to Sellafield imported nuclear waste train on 19th July 1996.

Photo: Dave Garrett

and 10,000 passengers per week (the second lowest band in the analysis), although a freight flow of around 50,000 tons per week was regarded as fairly healthy. Passenger traffic receipts at all stations between Barrow and Sellafield were in the lowest category at less than £5,000 per annum. Similarly, freight traffic tonnage at most of the coast line stations was in the lowest category of below 5,000 tons per annum, but the ironworks traffic handled at Millom put it into the middle band of between 5,000 and 25,000 tons per annum. Thankfully sanity eventually prevailed and the passenger service was retained, a decision influenced by the level of workmen's traffic to and from Sellafield and the necessity to keep the line open for Whitehaven, Sellafield and Millom freight.

In April 1966 all passenger trains between Barrow and Whitehaven went over to diesel multiple unit (DMU) operation, although this was not the first occasion that these trains, popular with passengers and staff alike, had been seen in Cumberland. BR's dieselisation policy had seen DMUs introduced on the Carlisle-Silloth line as early as 29th November 1954 and on the Whitehaven-Carlisle route, which saw conversion of its services on 7th February 1955. However steam still ruled on the through trains from Workington via Millom and Barrow to Carnforth and beyond. Following closely was the scenic Workington-Keswick-Penrith-Carlisle service, which was converted on 3rd March 1955. Plans to introduce DMUs between Whitehaven and Barrow were put forward in February 1955 but, in the event,

A Derby "Lightweight" unit, with one vehicle in the original green livery and the other in Rail Blue, heads towards the signal bracket carrying Millom's No 27 Up Home signal on 28th March 1968. Note the pink stains from the iron ore trains. The carriage shed was formerly situated over the siding nearest the cricket field.

Photo: Author

The Railway after 1923

Fowler 2-6-4T No 42376 has just cleared Limestone Hall crossing with the Up Mail. The setting sun glints on the loco and leading mail sorting van. By the time this photo was taken on 21st August 1961 mail was no longer dropped from the Whitehaven-Carnforth TPO and so the van has been marshalled with its letter rack side in view.

Photo: VR Webster/ Kidderminster Railway Museum

these were put on hold for another ten years until, on 1st March 1965, there was a partial changeover on Carnforth-Barrow-West Cumberland trains with some alterations to timings and the loss of the Liverpool through carriages. Modernisation may have been tentative in Furness and West Cumberland but elsewhere on BR the London Midland 25kV electrification was grabbing the headlines. Ironically, in the light of the April 1966 changes, the first ever Up train to arrive at London Euston behind an electric locomotive was the 06-38 ex-Workington (Millom depart 08-12) which arrived at 15-02 on 22nd November 1965. Full introduction of DMUs came with the start of the new timetable on 18th April 1966, using Derby "Lightweight" sets based at Carlisle and rendered surplus from the Workington-Keswick line, which had closed two days earlier. The downside of this change, however, was that the Barrow-Millom-Whitehaven service was reduced to a paltry five workings daily, although the proposed closure of Green Road and Silecroft stations to improve the viability of the DMU services did not go ahead. The arrival of the units coincided with the end of direct services from Workington to Euston and Manchester and the withdrawal of the Whitehaven to Euston sleeper north of Barrow; West Cumbrians had had little time to enjoy electric haulage of through coaches into the capital. The only regular passenger stock steam workings remaining were the morning and evening mail trains (the *Whitehaven-Stalybridge TPO* from 3rd January 1965 and *Whitehaven-Huddersfield TPO* from 2nd January 1966), which continued to be steam-hauled until 12th January 1968. In the early 1970s the Up TPO, which had not carried passengers since the arrival of the DMUs in April 1966, conveyed two coaches on Sundays only, mainly for the benefit of Ravenglass & Eskdale Railway volunteers needing to return to Millom and Barrow. The Sunday TPO ceased to run in May 1975 and the entire Whitehaven-Huddersfield operation ended on 28th September 1991.

Also dating from 1966 was a BR plan to single much of the Furness line between Carnforth and Whitehaven. Under this abortive scheme 500 yard long loops were to be installed on the single track at strategic locations. Foxfield would have had a loop and lay-by; Millom would have had a loop, lay-by, yard and the link to the ironworks; Silecroft would just have had the level crossing and Bootle would have had a loop, level crossing and yard. Fortunately this return to pre-1870s conditions never happened and the Carnforth-Sellafield section in 2012 still retains double track; Barrow North to Park South Junction has been singled, although the Barrow Avoiding Line remains double. Traditional semaphore signalling, with some colour lights, is still in evidence but the yards, planned for retention in 1966, are long gone.

In 1967 the Buccleuch Dock bridge in Barrow was declared unsafe. From 3rd July that year the long-running 06-20 (times varied by a few minutes over the years) Millom to Shipyard (Island Road) station and the 16-58 from Barrow Shipyard due to arrive in Millom at 17-38 were cut back to Barrow Central station, or *Barrow-in-Furness* as it was by then known, and a bus provided from there to the shipyard. The bus, effectively a rail-replacement service, only lasted until the official closure of Island Road on 7th October the following year, leaving the many Millom-based shipyard workers the choice of catching a service bus or walking.

Change was a characteristic of life in the 1960s and dramatic alterations to a century of railway practices round the Cumbrian Coast continued to be seen during 1967. From September most of the stations between Barrow and Whitehaven became unstaffed halts and the then-novel instruction given "Passengers wishing to alight must inform the guard and those wishing to join must give a hand signal to the driver." BR issued a dull little pamphlet, entitled *New Booking Arrangements Barrow-Whitehaven-Carlisle Line*, which informed would-be travellers that new booking arrangements were to come into operation on 4th September 1967. Fifteen ticket offices (including Foxfield, Green Road, Silecroft and Bootle, but not Millom) were to close and passengers would henceforth have to buy tickets from the guard. If passengers wished to travel beyond Barrow or Carlisle then they were informed of the necessity to rebook at these stations. Mr J Pollard, Divisional Manager at Preston, seemed to be preparing for the worst when, after explaining that the service had been unremunerative for many years, went on to reassure passengers:

It does not follow, however, that the service will automatically be withdrawn. Further steps are to be undertaken to cut costs in an endeavour to eliminate the losses. In any case, even if such a proposal were to be made at some time in the future, it would need to be dealt with in accordance with the procedures laid down in the Transport Act 1962, which among other things gives any user of the service so proposed for withdrawal the right to place an objection before the appropriate Transport Users Consultative Committee.

Mr Pollard made no comment on how ineffective such objections had been elsewhere in the case of the hundreds of line closures following the Beeching Report.

1968 saw further downgrading of facilities and from 19th May Millom booking office, while still remaining open, was limited to issuing tickets to stations between Barrow and Carlisle and to Euston, Lancaster, Preston and Manchester. Even this restricted service was not to last: from 18th July 1971 Millom was reduced to an unmanned halt, the ticket office closed and all staff withdrawn except on Mondays, when "special arrangements" were made for the sale of weekly season tickets from 06-00 to 07-55. The special arrangements involved a ticket clerk travelling to Millom on the empty stock of the first train to Barrow and so the large number of workmen travelling kept the ticket office going into the

1980s. At the same time the parcels and "luggage in advance" facilities were withdrawn, to leave Whitehaven and Workington the only stations between Barrow and Carlisle dealing with such business and selling tickets.

As related in Chapter 4, Millom Ironworks was in full production during the early BR period and this was reflected in buoyant inward and outward traffic flows. Moor Row shed closed in July 1954 but the remaining FR locos would travel light from Workington to work the Moor Row-Millom and Egremont-Millom trips. The Working Timetable from 20th September 1954 showed a 7-30am (Saturdays excepted) Moor Row to Millom and 2-30pm Egremont to Millom. The *Preston Division Trip Book from 18th April 1966 until further notice* showed Workington Targets 70 and 71, rostered for an Ivatt Class 4MT and Stanier Class 5MT respectively, bringing two trains of ore from Egremont to Millom. Target 70 left Workington at 05-00 and did five booked trips between Ullcoats and Egremont, before heading south at 15-20 to arrive in Millom at 16-45; departure with the empties was at 17-15, arriving at Egremont 18-35, from where the light engine worked back to Workington. On Fridays the timings varied, with the ore arriving in Millom at 14-15 and the empties returning at 15-05. The Class 5MT-worked turn departed from Workington light engine at 05-46, left Egremont at 07-36 and, after shunting at Sellafield and Bootle, arrived at Millom at 10-16; departure was at 11-15, when it worked light engine to Barrow for further passenger work. The iron ore trains were steam turns until the end of 1967 and in 1968, the final year of operation, Workington Targets 94 and 95 employed Clayton Type 1 (later Class 17) diesels on the daily pair of workings. Target 94 left Workington, light engine, at 05-10, Egremont at 07-25, shunted Sellafield and Bootle and arrived at Millom at 09-55: return was at 10-05, shunting Bootle and Vickers at Eskmeals, before arriving at Egremont for 11-55 and picking up stone from Rowrah to Derwent Ironworks at Moor Row. Target 95 left Workington at 04-40 and, after working between Ullcoats and Egremont as required, left the latter at 15-20 to arrive at Millom at 16-40: return was at 17-30, arriving at Egremont at 18-50 and departing light engine for Workington.

A Millom-Barrow weekly ticket of 1979. Sales of these tickets kept the Millom booking office open long after the others in the area had closed.

Author's Collection

In addition to receiving iron ore from Hodbarrow and Florence/Ullcoats, Millom Ironworks continued to import the mineral from Spain, Portugal and North Africa via Ramsden Dock at Barrow. During the 1950s and 1960s BR was moving two trains of imported ore from Barrow Docks to Millom daily, initially hauled by Fowler 4Fs and then by Stanier Class 5s. The *1966 Preston Division Trip Book* lists Ramsden Dock departures at 10-42 and 13-20, arriving at Millom at 11-39 and 14-16 respectively, although when iron ore was being unloaded

Furness 0-6-0 52499 passes the FR Home signal at clear as it nears journey's end with the 1-00pm Moor Row-Millom Class J Mineral on 9th September 1954. This loco was one of the handful of FR 0-6-0s which survived to serve the nationalised system but succumbed to the cutter's torch less than three years after this photograph was taken.

Photo: CRA Library Ref PEG290

The Railway after 1923

Stanier Class 5 45231 of Carnforth shed wheels a Class H freight towards Barrow on 25th June 1968. St George's spire is seen over the train, the Co-op in Wellington Street is the largest building on the left hand skyline and the 1959-built comprehensive school can be glimpsed on the right. Hodbarrow had closed three months earlier, the ironworks would finish in less than twelve weeks, 45231 would last until the end of steam in August and the Co-op would collapse in the following year - truly, the end of an era.

Photo: Author

at Barrow there could be more trains to handle the traffic and then nothing at all at other times. The Class 5s continued on these trains until June 1968, only two months before steam finally finished on BR and virtually to the end of importing ore through Barrow.

The ironworks consumed vast amounts of coke. There would be up to two days' supply of coke within the works, with Park and Foxfield sidings used as stabling points for full wagons when there was sufficient in the works or in Millom yard; thus BR regulated the supply and absorbed fluctuations in demand by either stabling or by direct delivery. Having arrived at Millom the coke wagons (initially wooden NER and LNER hoppers but gradually steel wagons after the mid-1930s) were worked down the Hodbarrow branch by the 'main line' locomotive to the ironworks sidings or the Hodbarrow Mineral Sidings on the Mains, from where they were worked to the ironworks as required. Coke from County Durham continued to be supplied via Stainmore and Lindal Ore Sidings, but in December 1959 the British Transport Commission announced proposals to close most of the Stainmore lines, including the route between Kirkby Stephen and Tebay. From 4th July 1960 the coke traffic, now down to two trains a day, was diverted over a 70-mile-longer route via the Newcastle and Carlisle line and the Cumbrian coast, although the link over the Pennines to Tebay did not finally close until 20th January 1962. From the 1950s, at least, Millom was using increasing quantities of coke from the West Riding of Yorkshire, and the 10-10am Millom to Lindal Ore Sidings was noted as being made up of Midland Railway and North Eastern Railway coke empties in the *Barrow Shunting Engine and Local Trip Notice 10th September 1951 until further notice*: note the use of pre-Grouping company names 28 years after they had ceased to exist. Relatively small tonnages of coke breeze (undersized screenings, typically less than half an inch) were obtained from Barrow and White Lund (Morecambe) gas works.

Once Redhills Quarry closed after the Second World War, Millom Ironworks relied on Goldmire Quarry, near Askam, for its limestone. The quarry was accessed from the Dalton Loop Line and cleared by a trip working from Barrow (Target 18 in the 1950s and Target 83 later) which transferred wagons to and from Park Sidings, from where they were tripped to and from Millom with the coke traffic. In 1951 British Railways listed Target 30

On 19th July 1961 Fowler LMS 4F 44487 shunts ironworks traffic on the Hodbarrow branch close to the end of the BR line at Crab Marsh. The loco had been a resident of Barrow shed since LMS days and would be withdrawn from there nine months later. Duddon Villa, the former home of Thomas Massicks, dominates the left skyline.

Photo: CRA Library Ref PES362

(Park Sidings-Millom Sidings-Millom Ironworks-Hodbarrow) as a Class 4F 0-6-0 turn although one of the remaining FR 0-6-0s, 52494 or 52509, occasionally strayed from Barrow to work this duty. The locomotive did four trips down the Hodbarrow branch to the ironworks and extended only the second one to the Hodbarrow sidings. By 1966 Target 81 involved a 350 hp diesel shunter arriving on Monday mornings from Barrow, shunting ironworks traffic during the week and returning to Barrow MPD on Saturday evenings; the terse instruction, "Daily immobilise locomotive at Millom from 19-40 to 07-00" explained what happened overnight. One unusual working on the Hodbarrow branch occurred on Sunday 27th August 1961 when *The Furness Railtour*, which had started from Manchester, ventured as far as the end of BR metals at the gate before the mineral sidings. Late in the afternoon 4F 0-6-0 44347 propelled the train back to the ironworks for an impromptu inspection of the fleet of locomotives. Leaving Millom almost an hour late at 5-25pm, the special did a trip up the Coniston branch before returning to Manchester.

The roadside goods trains which had served all stations between Barrow and Whitehaven were, like everywhere else on BR, in terminal decline by the early 1960s. Stations to the north were shunted by the 12-10pm Millom to Moor Row and those to the south by the 1-5pm (Saturdays excepted) or 1-38pm (Saturdays only) Millom to Barrow, according to the Local Trip Notice published by the Barrow Operating Superintendent's Office in September 1951. Only eight months after their closure had been recommended by Dr Beeching, the goods facilities at Green Road and Silecroft were shut down, along with Drigg and St Bees, on 2nd December 1963. Bootle followed on 8th September 1968. The facilities at Millom survived until 16th November 1970 and in the early 1980s the derelict goods shed was sympathetically converted to a supermarket by WBG, being opened as *The Millom Market* by Jack Cunningham, the local MP. It reopened in 1984 as Liptons, before being taken over in turn by Presto, Safeway, Morrisons, Somerfield and, most recently, by Tesco in 2009.

The Hodbarrow branch was closed beyond the ironworks on 12th August 1968, although this section was not officially taken out of use until 2nd May 1971. The last rail traffic, comprising the dismantled plant and structures, left the ironworks site in 1971 and on 1st February 1972 the Hodbarrow branch was taken out of use beyond the eastern end of Millom's Down platform. The branch and machine roads were taken out of use on the same date, the remains of the branch reverting to a 440 yard long siding. The loss of the ironworks traffic from sidings 1 to 3 to the south meant that the slip connection on the crossover between the Up and Down lines close to the signal box was redundant and was secured out of use from the same date. Many signals were removed and, on 8th April that year, the Down refuge sidings were shortened by 77 yards. By 1990 all that remained was a single Down siding and the crossover. These still exist in 2012 although the headshunt disappeared with the relaying of the crossover and connection to the running line in October 2006 and the siding has been further shortened to accommodate a footpath. Once the company trains to Albright & Wilson at Corkickle (Whitehaven) had finished in 1986, the only remaining freight traffic flows through Millom were short-lived "Speedlink" wagonload services, which ceased in 1991, and the still-extant spent reactor fuel trains to Sellafield. Since 1995 this latter has been in the hands of Direct Rail Services (DRS), a company created by British Nuclear Fuels Ltd, which now handles all the UK's nuclear flask traffic. On 3rd March 2000 a single load of scrap, destined for Liverpool Alexandra Dock, was loaded from the remaining Down siding and in 2009 another "one-off" traffic flow commenced: on 19th January DRS began its Millom aggregate delivery programme from Ghyll Scaur Quarry to Drigg for the Low Level Waste Repository being built there. Using an overnight possession after the regular services had finished, the 1,400 tonne trains, made up of two Class 66s and JNA bogie box wagons, were loaded standing on the main line to the east of the station and then worked to Workington docks to run round, before returning to Drigg. The contract ended with the last Workington-Drigg train on 11th May 2010.

This view, taken around 1970 from St George's church tower, depicts a Class 25 on a string of ballast wagons opposite the 1913 replacement signal box. Notice the turntable pit at the centre bottom of the picture. Additions since the earlier view are the Palladium to the left of centre and the extensive 1950s-built council housing estate in the centre. The castle and The Old Church are in the right distance with Millom Park beyond.
Photo: Stephe Cove Collection

The Railway after 1923

By the 1980s BR's service on the Barrow-Whitehaven line was hardly designed to encourage passengers; taking 1983-84 as an example, a Millom passenger had a choice of six weekday Provincial Sector trains to Carlisle and one as far as Bootle, while in the Up direction there were eight services to Barrow and a further two as far as Lancaster. Ten years later the timetable showed the same number of Carlisle trains and 13 to Barrow, emphasising the long-term importance of Millom-Barrow services for work and shopping.

On 2nd March 1997 Great Western Holdings took over the Cumbrian Coast services which were run by North Western Trains when first privatised. The company was later renamed *First North Western*. This franchise lasted until 12th December 2004 when it passed to the Serco-NedRailways-owned *Northern Rail*, who continue to operate services with ex-BR 153 and 156 units. The 11th December 2011 to 13th May 2012 timetable shows 14 Up departures from Millom, nine of which were for Barrow only, with the remaining five continuing to Lancaster or Preston. Most of the Up trains start from Carlisle. In the opposite direction a similar number of trains arrive, ten working Barrow-Carlisle services, one Barrow-Sellafield and three Barrow-Millom. Two Down trains start their journeys at Preston and two at Lancaster.

Major improvements, including new waiting shelters, landscaping and repainting were unveiled in May 1991, and in 1993 plans were announced to turn the redundant buildings into a crafts and social centre. This was to be a joint venture between the BR Community Unit, the Rural Development Commission and the European Regional Development Fund. The building is still owned by Network Rail but is leased to Copeland Borough Council who then sub-let it. Millom Folk Museum (now Millom Discovery Centre) moved into the station building in 2001 from premises adjacent to the library. The accommodation is shared with the Tourist Information Centre, tea room and the re-introduced railway booking office. Passenger usage remains buoyant, the number of passengers entering and leaving the station being around 220,000 per annum between 2006 and 2011. The other remaining stations between the Duddon and the Esk see considerably less use,

A packed platform of Sellafield workers awaits the early morning train at Millom in May 1991. Later that day the new shelters were formally opened.
Photo: Peter W Robinson

The Cumbrian Coast line continues to witness steam-hauled trains more than 40 years after the end of regular BR steam working. This view, taken on 5th May 1980, shows the Midland Compound No 1000 and Jubilee No 5690 Leander *on the* Royal Wessex *passing under the Moor Road bridge shortly after leaving Millom for Sellafield. The locos were deputising for the failed* Schools Class *Cheltenham.*
Photo: Frank Atkinson

Chapter Seven

Green Road averaging around 9,400 over the same period, Silecroft 9,600 and Bootle 15,500.

As the story of Millom and its railway has moved into the current century the dream of a Duddon crossing seems to be ever present, but the emphasis has shifted from a rail crossing to one for road traffic. In November 2001 Cumbria County Council agreed to drop its proposal for a £50 million Millom to Askam bridge following a feasibility study which highlighted a clash with environmental policies, poor value for money and a threat to the rail link. A spokesman said "The decision to stop pursuing the almost impossible concept would remove the uncertainty in transport planning for the area." Ten months later the saga started again at the instigation of road-biased councillors. In October 2004 a political party, *Build Duddon and Morecambe Bay Bridge Party*, was formed but got very little support in the following year's General Election and nothing has come of these proposals which were, inevitably, for road crossings. Most recently the 2007 publication by the Northwest Regional Development Agency, *Britain's Energy Coast/A Masterplan for West Cumbria*, showed a Duddon crossing as part of its aspirations. Apart from the appeal of an improved road (rail only features in a minor way in the report) link between Millom and Barrow, the opportunity to generate energy from the tidal flow in the estuary led to a £60,000 feasibility study. A change of government in 2010 and an economic downturn may well have set back such fanciful plans and so Hyde Clarke's plans of 1835 still remain unfulfilled.

Whilst the railway looks set to continue its 1850 route to cross the Duddon at Foxfield rather than from Hodbarrow Point, the shape of future passenger services makes for interesting speculation. At the time of writing, two new players are bidding to operate trains on the Cumbrian Coast: nuclear flask train operator DRS is investigating the possibility of running its own trains for Sellafield workers and Alliance Rail is proposing a Carlisle-London service via the coast, with Millom marked as one of its stops. Through coaches to London again after a 50 year gap? London to Scotland via Millom after 175 years?

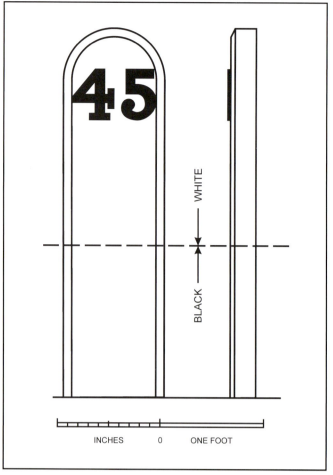

Furness Railway Milepost 45 at Millom station
Redrawn by Alan Johnstone from original drawing by Peter W Robinson.

Northern Rail Leyland single unit No 153 328 calls at Millom's Up platform with a Barrow train on 3rd August 2010. The 1991-built shelter is visible on the right and the 1913 signal box with its 21st century refurbishments controls the remaining semaphores.
Photo: Alan Johnstone Ref 10_5675

Appendix 1

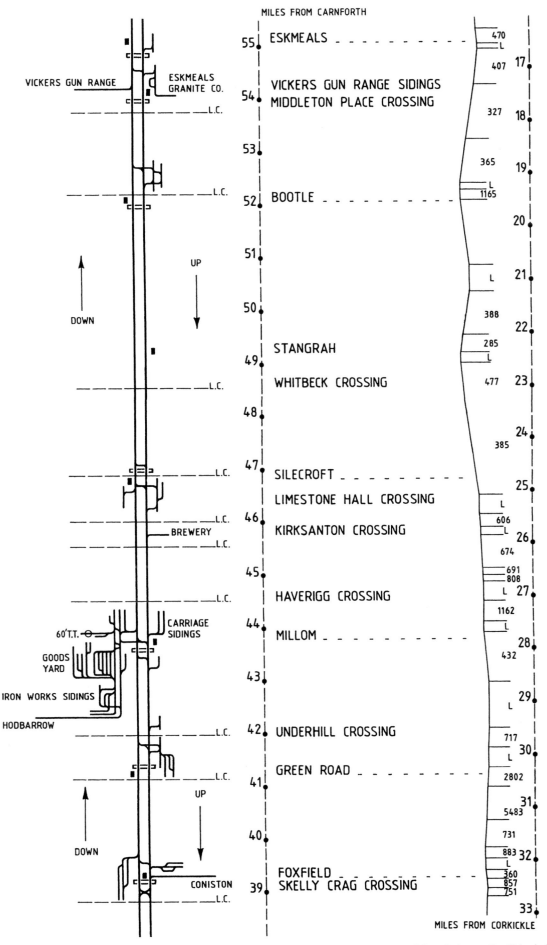

LMS Strip Map This extract from a line plan dated 8th June 1925 shows running lines and sidings between the Esk viaduct and Foxfield.
Drawn by Mike Faulkner, based on drawing in CRA Collection.

Appendix 2

The Rescue of Millom Ironworks No 1

Reprinted from Volume 10 No 10, May 2012 of *Cumbrian Railways*, the Journal of the Cumbrian Railways Association

AFTER MILLOM Ironworks closed on "Black Friday", 13th September 1968, various locomotives that had worked there were utilised by the scrap contractors engaged in the demolition of the works. Over a period of nearly two years the whole works was dismantled and shipped out in pieces from the pier or by rail until finally in July 1970 the last working locomotive, Millom No 1, an 0-4-0ST supplied new to Millom by Andrew Barclay in 1953 as Works Number 2333, finished moving scrap. The Receivers of Millom Hematite Ore and Iron Company Ltd handed over the site to Millom Investments Ltd on 20th January 1971 and the very last job carried out by No 1 for this latter company was to shunt the unique ex-Barrow Steel Works Peckett (Works Number 1895 of 1935) and the 1902-built Barclay (Works Number 929) on to the site of the old loco shed and workshop which had blown down many years previously. Track was then lifted, leaving the locos marooned.

In August 1971 Dr J Hubert Jackson, who was then works medical officer at Vickers at Barrow, bought No 1 from Millom Investments Ltd on the condition that he made himself responsible for moving it out of the works area. Hubert's intentions were to take the locomotive to the then-thriving steam centre at Steamtown, Carnforth to join the mixture of industrial and main line locomotives housed there. British Rail was prepared to haul the Barclay to Carnforth "subject to the locomotive being passed as fit to run on its own wheels" and the Divisional Manager at Preston quoted a figure of £85 for the trip.

Hubert's main problem was that, although No 1 was capable of steaming, there was over 400ft of track missing between the rails on which the loco was standing and the remainder of the works system. Undaunted, he and his wife Mary, assisted by brothers Joe, Harold and William Walker, set to work relaying the track and rebuilding two damaged sets of points. They then had to clear their way through a large scrap heap which covered their exit route to the Hodbarrow branch, the whole exercise taking some four weeks of night and weekend work and resulting in the clearance of some 200 tons of metal. To help clear a path through the heap they borrowed a crane from Mullhollands, the scrap merchants, but even then this task alone took two whole days.

On 13th September No 1's tanks were filled and the fire lit but the long period of inactivity resulted in an inability to make steam. The following day William cleaned out the boiler tubes and this time the loco was able to make sufficient steam pressure to be able to move over the once-only track with extreme caution. The first set of points was negotiated successfully and it was then forward over the second set which opened on to the old coal road but at this point No 1 became entangled with some of the cleared scrap. Once clear of the obstruction the loco shunted 60 or so wagons before heading off along the Hodbarrow branch towards Millom station, where it was stabled in the yard behind the Down platform.

Over the next four weeks Hubert and the Walker brothers prepared the Barclay for its epic journey over BR to Carnforth: an ashpan was fashioned by a local craftsman and the lower extensions to the buffer beams removed, the tanks were refilled and the loco oiled and greased. At 4-00am on a wet Monday 11th October, Hubert arrived in the station yard to light up the loco and was joined by Joe Walker an hour later. Joe had been the Locomotive and Transport Superintendent at the ironworks and was to join Hubert on the footplate for the journey on the main line. Shortly before 10-00am English Electric Type 4 No 330 arrived from Barrow with a brake van in tow and, following careful inspection by the BR staff, the saddle tank was passed fit to travel. The remains of the once-extensive Millom yard allowed the diesel to make up its short train and, with much whistling, the convoy was soon on its way at a stately 15 miles per hour. Stops were made in the Loop at Dalton Junction, Grange yard and Arnside (on the Sandside branch) but No 1 suffered very little overheating and there was still plenty of water in the tank when she arrived at Carnforth. Despite only being in light steam, the sight of a steam loco on the main line caused much interest all along the route and camera crews from BBC *Look North* and Border TV captured the event on film.

Millom Ironworks No 1, Andrew Barclay 2333 of 1953 with (from left to right), William, Harold and Joe Walker and Hubert Jackson.

Photo: JH Jackson Collection

The route through the scrap heap has been cleared to reveal the old coal road – No 1's route to freedom. The bogie bolster wagon in the background is sitting on the remains of the Hodbarrow branch. This wagon was later shunted out of the way by No 1.

Photo: JH Jackson Collection

In its final days at Millom, No 1 had been named *David* after Joe Walker's grandson and on 3rd September 1972 the 13-year-old officially named the smartly repainted loco at a Steamtown open day. After being sold to the Walker family, *David* moved to the Haverthwaite headquarters of the L&HR on 14th March 1978 and remains there still as a memorial to the efforts of Hubert and Joe in preserving one of the last tangible remains of the great ironworks at Millom.

As a footnote, the other Barclay, Millom No 12 (Works No 929 of 1902), also made it into preservation and is currently at a private site in Gloucestershire but Millom No 9, the last surviving inside cylinder Peckett 0-4-0, did not beat the cutting torch, succumbing in October 1972. This article is based on notes made by the late Hubert Jackson and newspaper cuttings of the time in his collection. I am grateful to Hubert's widow, Mary, for permission to use this material.

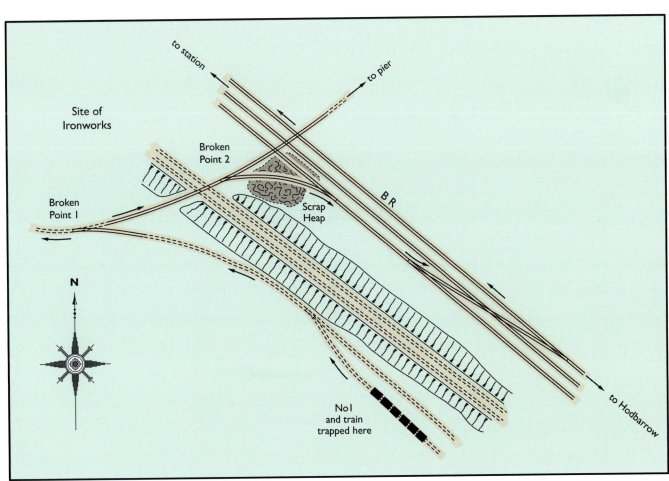

Map of Millom Ironworks site in September 1971 Solid lines represent rails still in place and dotted lines rails lifted. A bridge had been removed where rails on the embankment had crossed the line to the pier.

Map drawn by Alan Johnstone, from a sketch by Alan Atkinson based on information by JH Jackson.

At 11-20am on 11th October 1971 English Electric Type 4 No 330 leads No 1 and brake van under the A590 at Ruskinville bridge shortly before entering Dalton tunnel.

Photo: WL Mahoney, Collection of JH Jackson

British Railways quote for moving MIW No 1 from Millom to Carnforth.

JH Jackson Collection

Bibliography

Andrews, M: *The Furness Railway in and around Barrow* (Cumbrian Railways Association, 2003)

Andrews, M: *The Furness Railway, a History* (Barrai Books, 2012)

Barnes, F: *Barrow & District* (2nd Edition, Barrow Corporation, 1968)

Brown, DL: *A Brief History of the Eskmeals Gun Range* (Eskmeals, 1997)

Davies-Shiel, M & Marshall, JD: *Industrial Archaeology of the Lake Counties* (David & Charles, 1969)

Gilpin, L: *The Ulverstone & Lancaster Railway* (Cumbrian Railways Association, 2008)

Gradon, WM: *The Furness Railway: Its Rise and Development 1846-1923* (Author, 1946)

Harris, A: *Cumberland Iron* (Bradford Barton, 1970)

Jefferson, S: *The History & Antiques of Allerdale Ward above Derwent in the County of Cumberland* (1842)

Jewkes, J & Winterbottom, A: *An Industrial Survey of Cumberland & Furness* (Manchester University, 1933)

Joy, D: *A Regional History of the Railways of Great Britain Vol 14 The Lake Counties* (David & Charles, 1983)

Joy, D: *Cumbrian Coast Railways* (Dalesman, 1968)

Kelly, D: *The Red Earth* (Author, 1998)

Kelly, D: *The Red Hills* (Red Earth Publications, 1994)

Kirkham, R & van Zeller: P, *Rails round the Cumbrian Coast* (Dalesman, 1988)

Lancaster, JY & Wattleworth, DR: *The Iron & Steel Industry of West Cumberland* (British Steel Corporation, 1977)

Latham, T: *The Ashburner Schooners* (Ready Rhino, 1991)

Linton, J: *A Handbook of the Whitehaven & Furness Railway* (Whittaker, 1852)

Marshall, JD & Walton, JK: *The Lake Counties from 1830 to the Mid Twentieth Century* (Manchester University, 1981)

Marshall, JD: *Furness & the Industrial Revolution* (Barrow-in-Furness Library, 1958)

Melville, J & Hobbs, JL: *Early Railway History in Furness* (Cumberland & Westmorland Antiquarian & Archaeological Society Tract Series XIII, 1951)

Millom Hematite Ore & Iron Co Ltd: *Millom Hematite* (MHO&IC, 1959)

Myers, B: *Millom in Old Postcards* (2nd Edition, European Library, 1992)

Myers, B: *Millom in Old Postcards Volume 2* (European Library, 1994)

Myers, B: *Millom Remembered* (Tempus Publishing, 2004)

Nicholson, N: *Greater Lakeland* (Robert Hale, 1969)

Nicholson, N: *Portrait of the Lakes* (Robert Hale, 1963)

Nicholson, N: *Provincial Pleasures* (Robert Hale, 1959)

Nicholson, N: *Wednesday Early Closing* (Faber & Faber, 1975)

Norman, KJ: *The Furness Railway, Volumes 1 & 2* (Silver Link, 2001)

Pevsner, N: *The Buildings of England, Cumberland & Westmorland* (Penguin, 1967)

Quayle, H: *Whitehaven, The Railways & Waggonways of a Unique Cumberland Port* (Cumbrian Railways Association, 2007)

Rastrick, JU: *Report to the Provisional Committee of the West Cumberland, Furness & Morecambe Bay Railway* (Whitehaven, 1839)

Reed, B: *Crewe to Carlisle* (Ian Allan, 1969)

Rush, RW: *The Furness Railway* (Oakwood Press, 1973)

Stephenson, G: *Report to the Whitehaven Committee of the Caledonian Junction Railway* (Ulverston, 1837)

Taylor, Rev S: *The Story of the Old Church of the Holy Trinity, Millom* (British Publishing Company, 1936)

Tyler, I: *The Lakes & Cumbria Mines Guide* (Blue Rock, 2006)

Warriner, F: *Millom People and Places* (Author, 1937)

Warriner, F: *The Millom District, a History* (Author, 1932, republished Michael Moon, 1974)

Articles & Papers

Anderson, P: *Hodbarrow Iron Mines* (published in *Railway Bylines*, 2012)
Davis, DR: *Millom – the End Game* (published in *Master of them All: Iron Making in Cumbria*, Cumbria Industrial History Society, 2007)
Golding, C: *Destination Millom* (published in *British Railway Journal*, 2004)
Harris, A: *Millom: a Victorian New Town* (published in *Cumberland & Westmorland Antiquarian & Archaeological Society Transactions*, 1966)
Holland, E: *Hodbarrow Mine – Industry within an Industry* (published in *Master of them All: Iron Making in Cumbria*, Cumbria Industrial History Society, 2007)
Holland, E: *Hodbarrow Mines, Cumberland* (published in *Mine & Quarry Engineering*, 1962)
Hughes, R: *Millom – an Industrial Colony 1860-1875* (published in *Cumberland & Westmorland Antiquarian & Archaeological Society Transactions*, 2006)
Morgan, T: *Tugs of the Hodbarrow Mining Company* (published in *Marine News*, 1978)
Robinson, PW: *The Wartime Crisis on the Furness Railway* (published in *Backtrack*, 2005)
Tonks, ES & Barnes, S: *Dedicated?* (published in *Industrial Railway Record*, 1968)
Wilson, B: *Moor Row MPD* (published in *Railway Bylines*, 1998)
Winding, PF: *Traffic Divisions of British Railways – Barrow* (published in *Modern Railways*, 1965)

Acknowledgements

Although my name is on the cover, this book has come to fruition with the support and advice of many people whose efforts I am most happy to put on record.

Staff at the Cumbria Archives and Local Studies Centre at Barrow have been unstinting in their efforts to respond to my requests. Norman Gray and David Gibson received similar courtesy and patience when searching on my behalf at the Whitehaven and Carlisle centres.

The National Archives at Kew provided unfailing support in helping me access their vast resources, as did the staff of Worcestershire County Libraries in obtaining obscure volumes from their own and other catalogues.

Karen Pugh and her colleagues at the Millom Discovery Centre put their displays and huge reserve collection at my disposal. They could not have been more accommodating and readers are encouraged to visit the Centre at Millom Station to discover much more about the town's history than could be accommodated in these pages.

I am indebted to Mary Jackson, widow of Hubert Jackson, for her generous donation of his photographs and notes appertaining to the town's railway history. It is a source of great sadness that Hubert did not live long enough to see this volume in print and I hope he would have approved of the way I have incorporated the invaluable help and advice he gave me.

Bill Myers and Stephe(n) Cove are Millom residents who have given me the benefit of their in-depth local knowledge and free access to their photographic collections.

Peter Holmes is an acknowledged expert on Cumbrian industrial railways and locomotives. His collection of photographs has provided vast riches and the history of the Hodbarrow, Ironworks and Eskmeals railway systems could not have been written without his assistance.

Geoff Holme and Ron Herbert are former Cumbrian railwaymen whose professional knowledge, particularly with regard to signalling and operation, has been invaluable.

Lorraine Wilson provided me with much information on Brockbank's Brewery and the Whicham Mines.

Peter Robinson has spent a great deal of time sourcing photographs from his own and the Cumbrian Railways Association's collections. He has also used his skills to ensure that all the photographs in the book are suitable for publication. I must also thank David Postle at the Kidderminster Railway Museum for making available his vast photographic archive.

Alan Johnstone and Mike Faulkner have used considerable time and skill to produce the numerous maps and drawings contained herein. Alan has been unstinting in his efforts to convert my sketches into readable maps and to accommodate my frequent changes.

Thanks are due to Mike Peascod and the Cumbrian Railways Association Publications Team for the preparation of the book and to the numerous members and friends in the CRA whose collective knowledge of the County's railways has been indispensible. My thanks to Howard Quayle for his careful reading of the original text, for subsequently making further suggestions, and for his checking of the final version.

The Town Clerk and Councillors of Millom Town Council graciously gave permission to use the town's device to complement Alan Gunston's painting on the front cover. Finally, I would like to acknowledge the ongoing support of my wife, Jean, throughout this project. Her proof-reading skills are particularly appreciated.

I apologise for any names inadvertently missed from the list. Needless to say, any errors are mine and mine alone.

Alan Atkinson

Index

A
Accidents	70, 72, 76-81, 90, 91, 95, 96
Aird, John	34-36
Alquife Mines & Railway Co	47, 48, 51
Askam Ironworks	45, 47, 48, 70

B
Bank Springs Brewery	44, 45
Barratt, John	9, 27-29, 31, 59
Barrier, Inner	32-34, 36
Barrier, Outer	34-36, 66
Barrow Haematite Iron & Steel Co	9
Barrow Hematite Steel Co	48, 52
Beeching Report	97, 102
Black Combe	7, 11, 73, 91
Bootle	7, 13-15, 17, 66
Bootle Board of Guardians	59, 61, 63-66
Bootle station	17, 19, 20, 69, 71, 73, 95, 96, 99, 100, 102, 104
Borwick Rails	8, 24, 25, 28, 31, 69
Boyvill family	7
Brockbank, James Wilson and William	45
Brotherton & Rigg	16, 18

C
Caine, Nathaniel	9, 10, 26, 27, 29, 59, 62, 63
Clarke, Hyde	11
Co-operative Movement	61, 65, 66, 68
Cumberland Iron Mining & Smelting Co	10, 41-45, 59

D
Davis, James	9, 27
Duddon crossing	11-17, 22-25, 67-70, 91, 104
Duddon fords	7, 10, 19, 71
Duddon Furnace	9
Duddon sands	10, 11, 14, 19, 25, 68
Duddon Shipbuilding Co	31
Duddon Shipping Association	30, 31

E
Esk viaduct	12, 17, 19, 69
Eskmeals Granite Co	81, 86, 87
Eskmeals Gun Range	40, 81, 85-87, 95, 100
Eskmeals station	19, 20, 71, 72, 86

F
Fell & Joplin	16, 18
Florence mine	48-50, 52, 53, 91, 100
Foxfield	10, 17-19, 69, 70, 99, 104

G
Ghyll Scaur quarry	54, 66, 102
Goldmire quarry	45, 51, 93, 101
Green Road station	19, 21, 72, 77, 97, 102, 104

H
Hague, John	12-14
Haverigg	10, 34, 36, 59, 66-69
Hodbarrow branch	18, 23, 25, 26, 29, 40-43, 47, 58, 59, 69, 88, 95, 101, 102
Hodbarrow mine	9, 23, 26-40
Hodbarrow pier	25, 28-32, 39, 41, 54
Hodbarrow Point	12, 24, 38
Hodbarrow tugs	29, 30
Holborn Hill	10, 59, 61, 66
Holborn Hill station	19, 20, 25, 29, 59, 62
Huddleston family	7-9

I
Iron & Steel Corporation of Great Britain	39, 51

K
Kirksanton	7, 10, 44, 45

L
Lapstone Lodge	8, 19, 61-64
Lindal Ore Sidings	91, 93, 101
London Midland & Scottish Railway	91, 93-96
London & North Western Railway	26, 42, 47, 90, 91, 93, 95
Lonsdale, William, Second Earl	15, 17-19, 23, 25-27, 41, 45, 59, 64
Lowther, Sir James	8
Lowther, Sir William, First Earl of Lonsdale	10, 11, 27
Lucas & Aird	32, 34

M
Massicks, Thomas	31, 41, 45, 46, 55, 59, 63, 64
Millom & Askam Hematite Iron Co	45-51, 90
Millom castle	7, 8
Millom Hematite Ore & Iron Co	39, 52
Millom Ironworks	14, 41-58
Millom Ironworks pier	41-43, 47, 52, 54
Millom Local Board	41, 63-66
Millom Rural District Council	66, 67
Millom station	59, 61-63, 72-77, 94, 96-99, 102, 103
Millom Urban District Council	61, 66, 74, 76, 88
Millspray	52
Monk Moors halt	81, 85, 86
Morecambe Bay	11-15, 67, 68

N
Newtown	59-68, 74
North Lonsdale Iron & Steel Co	48, 50

P
Paley and Austin	63, 64, 69, 72-75
Park Sidings	93, 101, 102
Postlethwaite, William	31

R
Ramsden, James	9, 63, 64, 69
Rastrick, John Urpeth	13, 14
Redhills quarry	41, 45, 50, 93, 101
Rottington	8, 59, 60

S
Salthouse	10, 19
Schneider, Henry	9, 25, 59
Senhouse, Humphrey Le Fleming	11, 12
Signal boxes	77-85
Silecroft station	20, 22, 72, 81, 91, 92, 96, 99, 102, 104
Steel Green	27, 32, 36, 61, 67
Stephenson, George	11-16, 68

T
Thomas, William	31
Travelling Post Office	96, 99

U
Ullbank mine	46-48, 50
Ullcoats mine	47, 48, 50, 52, 53, 91, 100
Ulverstone & Lancaster Railway	14, 22
Underhill	9, 19, 21, 77

V
Vaughan, Cedric	32, 63, 66
Vickers Shipbuilding & Engineering	66, 68, 81, 85-88, 90, 95, 100

W
Waterblean mine	9, 10
West Cumberland Development Council	67
Whicham	7, 14, 16, 59, 66
Whicham Mining Co	44, 45
Whitbeck	7, 14, 19
Whitehaven Junction Railway	15, 16

Rear cover

Top
This postcard view, looking along Lapstone Road, shows the Conservative Club on the left. In the distance, Lancashire Road runs from left to right in front of the FR stables, beyond which is the goods shed with its characteristic semicircular windows. *Millom Discovery Centre Collection*

Left
In 1968 Millom's Down Distant, fixed at caution, comprised a Furness Railway wooden arm slotted in a lattice post with the spectacle plate mounted below the arm in order to improve sighting. *Photo: Author*

Middle right
On 20th April 1968 the fireman of Stanier 5MT 45394 ensures the tender is full before returning to Barrow with empty iron ore hoppers. Millom's turntable was out of use at this time and so a tender-first journey was necessary. *Photo: Author*

Lower right
A Barrow-bound Derby Lightweight DMU waits time at Millom in 1968. The first car has received the new Rail Blue livery but the other three still sport the original green. A Type 2-hauled Up freight is recessed beyond the signal box. *Photo: Author*